The Nonsense Verse of
EDWARD
LEAR

Edward Lear was born in 1812, the twentieth of twenty-one children. He began his professional career as a natural history illustrator and later became a prolific topographical landscape painter and draughtsman. He travelled widely and was the author of several travel journals. He produced humorous drawings all his life. His nonsense volumes include: *A Book of Nonsense* (1845); *Nonsense Songs, Stories, Botany and Alphabets* (1871); *More Nonsense, Pictures, Rhymes, Botany etc.* (1871); and *Laughable Lyrics* (1877). He died in 1888.

John Vernon Lord was born in 1939 and studied at the Salford School of Art and the Central School of Art and Design. Since the early 1970s he has devoted most of his illustrating time to children's books. He has collaborated with a number of established writers and has written and illustrated titles of his own, of which the best known is The Giant Jam Sandwich. *For seven years he was head of the Department of Visual Communication at Brighton Polytechnic, where he now teaches illustration on the Graphic Design course. He lives in London.*

METHUEN HUMOUR CLASSICS

Charles Addams
ADDAMS AND EVIL

Alphonse Allais
A WOLF IN FROG'S CLOTHING
Selected, translated and introduced by Miles Kington

H. M. Bateman
THE MAN WHO . . . AND OTHER DRAWINGS

Noël Coward
THE LYRICS OF NOËL COWARD
A WITHERED NOSEGAY

A. P. Herbert
UNCOMMON LAW
MORE UNCOMMON LAW

Paul Jennings
GOLDEN ODDLIES

Jerome K. Jerome
THREE MEN IN AN OMNIBUS

Osbert Lancaster
THE LITTLEHAMPTON SAGA

Tom Lehrer
TOO MANY SONGS BY TOM LEHRER

Frank Muir and Denis Norden
THE COMPLETE AND UTTER 'MY WORD!' COLLECTION

Ogden Nash
CANDY IS DANDY: THE BEST OF OGDEN NASH

S. J. Perelman
THE MOST OF S. J. PERELMAN
THE LAST LAUGH

W. C. Sellar and R. J. Yeatman
1066 AND ALL THAT
AND NOW ALL THIS

James Thurber
LET YOUR MIND ALONE!
THE MIDDLE-AGED MAN ON THE FLYING TRAPEZE

The Nonsense Verse of
EDWARD
LEAR

Illustrated by

JOHN VERNON LORD

A METHUEN HUMOUR CLASSIC

also by John Vernon Lord

THE TRUCK ON THE TRACK
with verses by Janet Burroway

THE GIANT JAM SANDWICH
with verses by Janet Burroway

THE RUNAWAY ROLLER SKATE

MR MEAD AND HIS GARDEN

WHO'S ZOO
poems by Conrad Aiken

MISERABLE AUNT BERTHA
with verses by Fay Maschler

A METHUEN HUMOUR CLASSIC

First published in Great Britain in 1984
by Jonathan Cape Ltd
This paperback edition first published in 1986
by Methuen London Ltd
11 New Fetter Lane, London EC4P 4EE
Introduction and illustrations Copyright © 1984 by John Vernon Lord

Made and printed in Great Britain

British Library Cataloguing in Publication Data

Lear, Edward
    The nonsense verse of Edward Lear. —(A
    Methuen humour classic)
    I. Title   II. Lord, John Vernon
    821'.8   PR4879.L2

ISBN 0-413-58390-2

For Denie

CONTENTS

ACKNOWLEDGMENTS

I am grateful to Brighton Polytechnic for granting me a six-month sabbatical period which offered me the time necessary for launching the project and reading and studying Lear's published journals and letters as well as most of the existing publications about his life and work. I have received valuable encouragement from friends and am indebted to the patience and support given to me by my family, who saw very little of me during four summers. For loyal support and backing from the beginning I owe much to Jonathan Cape Ltd, who have always given thoughtful advice and help.

The following are thanked for their permission to include copyright material: Harvard University Press, for the extract from Lear's diary on p. xv, which is reprinted from *Edward Lear as a Landscape Draughtsman* by Philip Hofer, published by the Belknap Press of Harvard University Press in 1967; the Houghton Library, Harvard University, for allowing us to reprint poems and limericks from manuscripts in its possession as follows: 'There lived a Small Puppy at Narkunda' on p. 136, 'There was an Old Man of Narkunda' on p. 136, 'There was a Small Child of Narkunda' on p. 136, 'She sits upon her Bulbul' on p. 162, 'Oh dear! How disgusting is life!' on p. 162, and 'The Uncareful Cow' on p. 199; H. P. Kraus, Rare Books and Manuscripts, for allowing us to reproduce the limericks, 'There was an Old Person of Leith' on p. 44, 'There was an Old Man of Orleans' on p. 46, 'There was an Old Man of the Dee' on p. 48, 'There was an Old Man who forgot' on p. 64 and 'There was an Old Man of the Cape' (variant) on p. 190, which are taken from *Lear in the Original* with an introduction and notes by Herman W. Liebert, published by H. P. Kraus, New York, in 1975; John Murray (Publishers) Ltd, for permission to reproduce the following material from *Teapots and Quails and Other New Nonsenses by Edward Lear*, edited and introduced by Angus Davidson and Philip Hofer, copyright © 1953 by John Murray: 'There was an Old Man of Carlisle' on p. 38, 'There was an Old Man of Girgenti' on p. 42, 'There was a Young Man in Iowa' on p. 58, 'There was an Old Person of Diss' on p. 76, 'There was an Old Person of Harrow' on p. 82, 'There was an Old Person of Brussels' on p. 113, 'There was an Old Man of the hills' on p. 115, 'Teapots and Quails' on pp. 180–3, 'There was an Old Person of Twickenham' on p. 201, 'There was an Old Person of Bradley' on p. 206, 'There was an Old Person of Cheam' on p. 207, 'The Scroobious Pip' on pp. 218–20 and 'Cold are the Crabs' on p. 223; the

ACKNOWLEDGMENTS

Trustees of the National Library of Scotland, for allowing us to use the text of 'The Pobble who has no Toes' (alternative version) on pp. 24–5, which is taken from a manuscript (MS. 3310, f. 14) in the Library's possession, and was first printed in Angus Davidson's *Edward Lear: Landscape Painter and Nonsense Poet*, published in 1938 by John Murray; the New York Public Library, for 'There was an Old Man whose giardino' which is reprinted on p. 110 with permission from Lola L. Szladits and Harvey Simmonds's *Pen and Brush: The Author as Artist*, copyright © 1969 by the New York Public Library, Astor, Lenox and Tilden Foundations; the Estate of Eric Partridge, controlled by Anthony Sheil Associates Ltd, for the incomplete fragment of 'The Children of the Owl and the Pussy-cat' on p. 6; Penguin Books Ltd, for permission to reprint 'There was an Old Man who made bold' on p. xv, which comes from p. 79 of *Edward Lear: Bosh and Nonsense*, published by Allen Lane in 1982, copyright © 1982 by the Trustees of Mrs C. H. A. M. Anstruther-Duncan; Miss M. H. Prescott, for allowing us to reprint 'There was an Old Man with a book' on p. 194, from the original which was sent by Edward Lear in a letter to Mr W. G. Prescott at Clarence, Roehampton; the Principal and Fellows of Somerville College, Oxford, for the lines 'Eating meat is half the battle' to 'as Lemons in your head!' which appeared in a letter of July 14th, 1883 from Edward Lear to Miss Amelia B. Edwards, A.B.E. 98, and which are reprinted in the poem 'Mrs Jaypher' on p. 153.

INTRODUCTION

Saith the Poet of Nonsense
'Thoughts into my head do come
Thick as flies upon a plum.'

(Lear writing to Carlingford,
from *Later Letters of Edward Lear*)

Edward Lear thought that the title 'Grand Peripatetic Ass and Boshproducing Luminary' ought to be conferred upon him by Prime Minister Gladstone; he also felt that Queen Victoria might honour him among the peerage as 'Lord High Bosh and Nonsense Producer'. But, as well as making him 'Derry down Derry', the 'Poet of Nonsense', Lear's creative talents encompassed a wide range of activities.

As an artist he produced humorous drawings all his life, mainly as a pastime, but he began his professional career as a natural history illustrator. Later, and from then on, he became a prolific topographical landscape painter and draughtsman. Besides writing nonsense he was the author of several travel journals and was an indefatigable letter-writer who corresponded with no fewer than 'four hundred and forty-four individuals in all'; sometimes writing as many as thirty-five letters before breakfast. Lear could also speak several languages. Furthermore (although his name does not yet grace the current edition of Grove!) he composed and sang tunes to his own 'vamping' accompaniment on the piano, much to the delight of Tennyson.

Perhaps the following brief account of Edward Lear's life will serve to introduce the general reader to the author of the famous poems and limericks. He was born in Holloway, North London on May 12th, 1812, the twentieth of twenty-one children. His father, Jeremiah, was a stockbroker who fell on hard times when Lear was a young boy. His parents had very little involvement in his upbringing and it was left to Edward's eldest sister, Ann, to look after him during his childhood and adolescence, as well as to help where she could with his basic education.

From childhood Lear suffered from asthma and bronchitis, the deep-rooted effects of which are apparent in his writings:

> Or grasping hard for breath do sit
> Upon a brutal chair,
> For to lie down in Asthma fit
> Is what I cannot bear.

> Or sometimes sneeze: and always blow
> My well-developed nose
> And altogether never know
> No comfort nor repose.

Moreover, throughout his life he was plagued by the 'Terrible Demon', the name he gave to his frequent bouts of epilepsy. He was also afflicted by regular depressions which he called 'the Morbids' or 'knownothingatallaboutwhat-oneisgoingtodo-ness'.

Ann and another sister, Sarah, had encouraged him to draw and paint natural history subjects in his early years and he began to make a living as an artist at the age of fifteen. Throughout the 1830s Lear was kept busy drawing and painting magnificent portraits of wildlife subjects for beautifully produced volumes. During this period he also carried out a number of commissions for the Derby family, depicting the various creatures that inhabited the Knowsley menagerie and aviary near Liverpool.

It was at Knowsley that Lear began to write and illustrate his nonsense verse for the Derby children. As a model he adopted a rhyming form which had already been used in two volumes published in the early 1820s. *The History of the Sixteen Wonderful Old Women* includes a verse with a familiar ring about it:

> There was an Old Woman named Towl,
> Who went to Sea with her Owl,
> But the Owl was Sea-sick, and scream'd for Physic;
> Which sadly annoy'd Mistress Towl.

The other volume, which Lear himself described as having 'a form of verse lending itself to limitless variety for Rhymes and Pictures', was *Anecdotes and Adventures of Fifteen Gentlemen*. In one of the verses in this edition the following unlikely situation arises:

> As a little fat man of Bombay
> Was smoking one very hot day,
> A bird called a snipe flew away with his pipe,
> Which vexed the fat man of Bombay.

However, it was not until some ten years or more after his Knowsley period that Lear's own 'absurdities' were immortalised in the publication of a book.

His health had never been good, and when in his mid-twenties his eyesight began to deteriorate, he was prompted to give up the demands of such detailed work as the fastidious description of wild and zoological creatures – parrots, pheasants, ducks, owls, monkeys, trogons, tortoises, terrapins and turtles. After visiting and making sketches in Ireland, the Lake District, Devon and Cornwall, Lear resolved to pack up his bags and become a traveller and landscape artist.

In 1837 he set off for Italy and by the end of the year had reached Rome, where he was based on and off for the next ten years, with sporadic visits to England and tours round Southern Italy. The year 1841 marked the publication of his first travel book *Views in Rome and its Environs*, which included a set of splendid lithographs.

The year 1846 was an *annus mirabilis* for Lear, in which he proved his versatility with three entirely different and highly successful publications. *Illustrated Excursions in Italy* included descriptions and landscape drawings of his recent travels; whilst *Gleanings from the Menagerie and Aviary at Knowsley Hall*, comprising natural history illustrations, and his *Book of Nonsense*, a collection of absurd verses with sparklingly original illustrations, represented the dual fruits of his labour and leisure at Knowsley. Furthermore, in the summer of the same year he was invited to give Queen Victoria a short course of drawing lessons, on the strength of Her Royal Highness's admiration for his drawings in the recently published *Illustrated Excursions*. The lessons were a success: she thought that he taught 'remarkably well' and he thought that Her Majesty was 'a dear and absolute duck'.

Lear's restless peregrinations following this period later resulted in two further travel books. *Journals of a Landscape Painter in Greece and Albania, &c.* (1851) included a collection of lithographs and descriptions of the places he had visited from late 1848 to mid 1849. *Journals of a Landscape Painter in Southern Calabria, &c.* (1852) described his earlier tours of Sicily, Calabria and the Kingdom of Naples.

He returned to England in the summer of 1849 and there he remained for four and a half years. With the help of a small legacy, his financial situation was healthy enough for him to undertake a course of study at the Royal Academy Schools. Here the bumbling 37-year-old bachelor (Her Majesty's drawing master and the author of the *Book of Nonsense*, no less!) drew from the antique alongside students almost half his age, hoping to improve his figure drawing and gain further skills in painting.

Lear spent most of his time in England painting in London and exhibiting his work, and preparing the travel books. He also visited his sister Ann and, being a popular and outgoing person, enjoyed the company of many friends. Some of these held high positions and, besides being constant companions, became dependable patrons as well as assisting him during periods of financial difficulty. Lear never married, although there is evidence in his writings that he was greatly preoccupied by the idea of marriage. He had believed himself in love when, at the age of 43, he met a half-English, half-Italian girl called Helena Cortazzi in Corfu, but this attachment fizzled out and some time later, in 1858, he wrote to his friend Fortescue, 'At 103 – I may marry possibly.' Lear contemplated marriage again in the mid 1860s. Gussie Bethel was the daughter of a friend and was considerably younger than himself. Again he had qualms and finally decided that the age difference, together with the financial problems that marriage would no doubt incur, were sufficient reasons to abandon the   xiii idea. Why, he thought, should she saddle herself with a feeble and fat old man? The connection between his tentative ideas on marriage and the heart-rending poem, 'The-Yonghy-Bonghy-Bò', is well known. The symbolism is revealed with poignant directness and simplicity – it is a tale of unrequited love:

> I am tired of living singly, –
> On this coast so wild and shingly, –
> I'm a-weary of my life;
> If you'll come and be my wife,
> Quite serene would be my life!

Lear continued to wander like the Dong upon the solitary plain, never to find his Jumbly girl.

After 1853 he lived abroad for the rest of his life with occasional visits to England. He stayed variously in Italy, Corfu and Cannes, finally making his home at San Remo in 1871. His time was spent in ceaseless wandering, painting and drawing as he did so, mainly in Italy, Malta, Egypt, Corfu, Albania, Greece and the Near East. Lear also toured India and Ceylon in 1873–4. He published *Views in the Seven Ionian Islands* in 1863 and *Journal of a Landscape Painter in Corsica* in 1870. The 1870s saw the publication of three more nonsense books: *Nonsense Songs, Stories, Botany and Alphabets* (1871), *More Nonsense* (1872) and *Laughable Lyrics* (1877).

Lear's journeys and explorations are recorded vividly in his hundreds of drawings and the published travel journals, which give an insight into the hazardous conditions he experienced as landscape painter and draughtsman. A moving account of this ailing and lonely old man in his early sixties is given in the posthumous publication *Edward Lear's Indian Journal*, edited by Ray Murphy (1953). As a ceaseless traveller Lear was constantly submerging himself in a welter of activity and he released much of his bustling and neurotic energy in the excited anticipation of new vistas which he avidly depicted and recorded as painter/draughtsman and writer. Travel was a way of overcoming his unpredictable health and moods and, even though he had plenty of friends, he was probably a loner at heart, preferring to communicate with them from a distance through the relative safety of letter-writing. Lear was also escaping; not to any place in particular, but in an effort to forget what he had left behind. On his intermittent visits to England he was not just returning home: Lear was escaping to England exactly as he had escaped from it. His attitude to life is mirrored in the predicaments of his nonsense subjects:

> There was an Old Man whose despair
> Induced him to purchase a hare:
> Whereon one fine day, he rode wholly away,
> Which partly assuaged his despair.

To try to escape is not the answer, but neither do Mr and Mrs Discobbolos have the solution to the problem of living in the world. In an attempt to flee from the worry of life they live for twenty years and more on top of a wall, until they realise that to isolate themselves like this is no remedy. The poem ends violently (as do a good number of the limericks), with the extinction of the Discobbolos clan. There is a pervasive sense throughout of 'the world having all gone wrong', to use the words of Mr Daddy Long-Legs and Mr Floppy Fly.

When he finally settled in San Remo, the last years of Lear's life appear to have been clouded with general ill health and melancholy, and he devoted much effort at this time to a vain attempt to produce over a hundred landscape illustrations for Tennyson's poems. Not long after the death of his faithful manservant, Giorgio Kokali, Lear wrote his last well-known nonsense poem, 'Uncle Arly', in 1884. Finally he was left quite alone when his daily companion, Foss, the seventeen-year-old cat, died. A few months later, on January 29th, 1888, Edward Lear himself died. Some weeks before he had written the final entry in his diary:

> Dreariness . . . [yet] out of doors bright sun. Looking over journals for 1887. Weary work . . . I shall try to get some sleep if possible, but I have no light or life left in me, – and the flies are as horrible as ever.

For the reader wishing to know more about the life of Edward Lear there are two major biographical studies: the pioneer work by Angus Davidson which was first published in 1938, and the more recent excellent and sympathetic study by Vivien Noakes, *Edward Lear: The Life of a Wanderer*, first published in 1968 with a revised edition later made available in paperback.

Lear's experience of life is woven into the fabric of his nonsense and there may be layers of underlying meanings in his writing. Much has been written about how his loneliness, restlessness and despair are expressed in his nonsense literature and how his representation of the individual in combat against society (with its 'nosy-parkers', pressure-groups and bureaucrats) is manifested through the 'they' of his limericks. Quite apart from the poignant and poetic qualities of his work, it stands on its own as pure nonsense; moving though much of his poetry is, it is also absurd.

The absurd nature of his nonsense thrives on being encapsulated within the strict formal structure of the limerick. Lear's limericks are thought by some to be feeble, on the grounds that the rhyming word in the last line repeats the rhyme in the first or second line. There are many who prefer a 'fresh' rhyming word in the last line so that it acts like the punch-line in a joke.

There are in fact five limericks included in this book that do have a third-word rhyme in the last line: the 'Old Man of the Coast'; the 'Young Lady whose eyes'; the 'Old Lady whose folly'; the 'Old Man who forgot' and the 'Old Man who supposed'. There are a handful more that also use a fresh rhyme, from the newly discovered set of 79 published in *Edward Lear: Bosh and Nonsense*. The understatement in the last line of one of these limericks is delightful:

> There was an Old Man who made bold,
> To affirm that the weather was cold:
> So he ran up & down, in his grandmother's gown –
> Which was woollen, & not very old.

The fact that there are precursors to Lear's limericks which included three different rhyming words, and that he himself had experimented with the technique, leads one to believe that his choice of repeating the same word particularly suited his own needs of expression. Perhaps the repeated rhyme had a distinct purpose in the aural tradition of telling stories and nursery rhymes in Victorian times. Maybe the nature of Lear's limericks was influenced by the presence of children eager to join in a chorus on the predictable 'home key' of the final words.

A look through a number of well-known anthologies of nonsense, light, comic and curious verse, as well as books of quotations, reveals that the inclusion of the fresh rhyming-word limericks by Lear is very rare indeed. Those limericks which seem to crop up most frequently are: the 'Old Man with a beard' (where birds built their nests); the 'Old Man who said "Hush!" '; the 'Old Man of Thermopylae'; the 'Young Lady of Ryde'; the 'Young Lady of Tyre' and the 'Old Man of Cape Horn', all of which culminate with a repeated, rather than a fresh, rhyming word. In his introduction to *The New Oxford Book of Light Verse* Kingsley Amis admits to including four of Lear's limericks 'with reluctance'; yet curiously enough, those which he selects are versions with the repeated rhyme in the last line – the very ones he considers should be 'best avoided'.

The echoing effect of Lear's repeated rhyme-words often maintains and enhances the feeling of non-sense, leaving the limerick subjects in a perpetual state of suspended animation (even those whose lives are concluded). The denouements flatten us with their inconsequential outcome, allowing many of his plots to thin as well as thicken. We are simultaneously involved in the predicament of his characters, and yet detached from them as the sense escapes us. We are moved and unmoved.

Lear's rich narrative convincingly transports us to his land of Nonsense through the evocative lyricism in the longer poems on the one hand, and the compactness of the limericks on the other. The essence of his language is to be found in the rhythm of his verse and the melodic use of words which manage to convey a sense of real feelings and an idea of non-sense at the same time.

I am only too aware that it is somewhat bold to attempt to illustrate Edward Lear's nonsense verse when his own drawings are so highly regarded. Many will feel that they should be left well alone and that there is no point in re-doing what has already been done with inimitable *finesse* by the author himself. There will be some Lear enthusiasts, accustomed to viewing Lear's own drawings alongside his verse, who may find that my efforts will taint, or even distort their vision of Lear's creations. The illustrations in this edition are the result of a long-lasting enthusiasm for Lear's work and I hope that my interpretations may provide a new perspective for those already acquainted with his artistry. At the same time I hope the book, which is intended for readers of all ages, will contribute generally towards a further spread of interest in Lear.

This collection of Lear's nonsense verse is mostly selected from the four volumes of nonsense published during the author's lifetime, supplemented by a group of posthumous publications. The sources from which the poems have been gathered are listed at the end of the book. Apart from *Nonsense Stories,*

Cookery and *Alphabets*, which have been omitted, this is a comprehensive collection of Lear's nonsense verse, and includes some material that is currently out of print. His *Nonsense Botany* and *Flora Nonsensica* have been incorporated in the endpapers.

Counting the 'Narkunda' three-versed poem as one limerick and including 'Derry down Derry', there are 236 illustrated limericks here. At the time of writing, I believe this volume represents the most extensive collection of Lear's limericks yet published. There are a number of variants of the wording and, with one or two exceptions, the most familiar rendering has been used.

Just as the illustrations for this book were being completed a fresh set of limericks happily came to light. This newly discovered group of 79 limericks and illustrations was published in *Edward Lear: Bosh and Nonsense* by Allen Lane in 1982. These were found among the Duncan papers in Naughton House, Fife, and about three-quarters of them are similar to or are variants of the texts included in this collection. However, there is among the 79, a number of entirely new limericks as well as some with significantly improved variants, which I would have liked to have included here had time allowed.

There has been an attempt to maintain some sort of consistency in the punctuation of verses in this edition, as not all Lear's original manuscripts are available and published editions of his work vary considerably. Lear himself was by no means consistent in his use of capital letters and, on the whole, there doesn't seem to be any particular significance in his choice between capital and lower-case letters. The limericks here have been presented in four-line stanzas, though lovers of the form *per se* often prefer the five-line presentation. There is evidence from Lear's own manuscripts that he had a tendency to write his limericks in two or three lines; there are also instances when he set them out in four or five lines.

The limericks have been arranged into loosely connected themes which bring together some of the topics that preoccupied Lear. The subjects with remarkable noses, the dancers, the greedy ones, the ones who spend their time in trees, and other related limerick personae, have been placed together in order to throw light on one another.

There are occasions when Lear, in his own illustrations, parodies the similarities between the limerick subjects and the beasts with which they associate. For example, the Old Man of El Hums resembles his fellow crumb-eating birds and the Old Person of Ems, despite the fact that he drowns in the Thames, looks remarkably like a fish. Lear also likes making other kinds of visual jokes: in his drawing of the Old Man of Ancona he depicts a small dog as an exceedingly large one, and it is difficult to discern whether the Old Man on a Hill is actually on a hill, as Lear teasingly depicts the flattest of surfaces. I have tried to avoid doing the same, unless it is suggested in the text, as I feel that this kind of visual humour is the special preserve of Lear. Of course, I would not deny that Lear's influence is apparent in certain aspects of my approach to illustrating his texts. However, I would like to think that my illustrations are able to speak for themselves.

John Vernon Lord

January 1984

There was an Old Derry down Derry,
Who loved to see little folks merry;
So he made them a Book, and with laughter they shook
At the fun of that Derry down Derry.

1

The Owl and the Pussy-cat

The Owl and the Pussy-cat went to sea
  In a beautiful pea-green boat,
They took some honey, and plenty of money,
  Wrapped up in a five-pound note.
The Owl looked up to the stars above,
  And sang to a small guitar,
'O lovely Pussy! O Pussy, my love,
    What a beautiful Pussy you are,
      You are,
      You are!
  What a beautiful Pussy you are!'

Pussy said to the Owl, 'You elegant fowl!
  How charmingly sweet you sing!
O let us be married! Too long we have tarried:
  But what shall we do for a ring?'
They sailed away, for a year and a day,
  To the land where the Bong-tree grows
And there in a wood a Piggy-wig stood
    With a ring at the end of his nose,
      His nose,
      His nose,
  With a ring at the end of his nose.

2

'Dear Pig, are you willing to sell for one shilling
   Your ring?' Said the Piggy, 'I will.'
So they took it away, and were married next day
   By the Turkey who lives on the hill.
They dined on mince, and slices of quince,
   Which they ate with a runcible spoon;
And hand in hand, on the edge of the sand,
   They danced by the light of the moon,
       The moon,
       The moon,
They danced by the light of the moon.

4

The Children of the Owl and the Pussy-cat

(AN INCOMPLETE FRAGMENT OF A SEQUEL TO 'THE OWL AND THE PUSSY-CAT')

Our mother was the Pussy-cat, our father was the Owl,
And so we're partly little beasts and partly little fowl,
The brothers of our family have feathers and they hoot,
While all the sisters dress in fur and have long tails to boot.
    We all believe that little mice,
      For food are singularly nice.
Our mother died long years ago. She was a lovely cat
Her tail was 5 feet long, and grey with stripes, but what of that?
In Sila forest on the East of far Calabria's shore
She tumbled from a lofty tree – none ever saw her more.
Our owly father long was ill from sorrow and surprise,
But with the feathers of his tail he wiped his weeping eyes.
And in the hollow of a tree in Sila's inmost maze
We made a happy home and there we pass our obvious days.

From Reggian Cosenza many owls about us flit
And bring us worldly news of which we do not care a bit.
We watch the sun each morning rise, beyond Tarento's strait;
We got out ——————— before it gets too late;
And when the evening shades begin to length from the trees
    ——————— as sure as bees is bees.
We wander up and down the shore ————————
Or tumble over head and heels, but never, never more
Can see the far Gromboolian plains ————————
Or weep as we could once have wept o'er many a vanished scene:
This is the way our father moans – he is so very green.

Our father still preserves his voice, and when he sees a star
He often sings —— to that original guitar.
——————————————

——————————————

The pot in which our parents took the honey in their boat,
But all the money has been spent, beside the £5 note.
The owls who come and bring us news are often——
6   Because we take no interest in poltix of the day.

There was an Old Man with a ribbon,
Who found a large volume of Gibbon,
Which he tied to his nose, and said, 'I suppose
This is quite the best use for my ribbon.'

There was an Old Man of Dunrose;
A parrot seized hold of his nose.
When he grew melancholy, they said, 'His name's Polly,'
Which soothed that Old Man of Dunrose.

There was an Old Man with a nose,
Who said, 'If you choose to suppose,
That my nose is too long, you are certainly wrong!'
That remarkable Man with a nose.

There was an Old Man, on whose nose,
Most birds of the air could repose;
But they all flew away, at the closing of day,
Which relieved that Old Man and his nose.

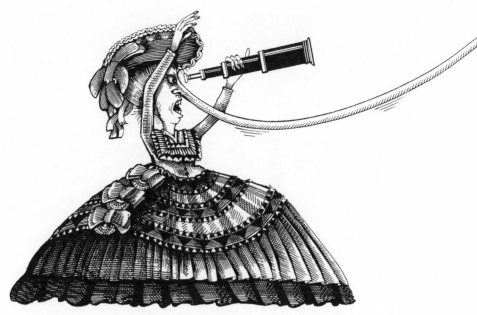

There is a Young Lady, whose nose,
Continually prospers and grows;
When it grew out of sight, she exclaimed in a fright,
'Oh! Farewell to the end of my nose!'

There was a Young Lady whose nose,
Was so long that it reached to her toes;
So she hired an Old Lady, whose conduct was steady,
To carry that wonderful nose:

9

There was an Old Man of West Dumpet,
Who possessed a large nose like a trumpet;
When he blew it aloud, it astonished the crowd,
And was heard through the whole of West Dumpet.

There was an Old Person of Cassel,
Whose nose finished off in a tassel;
But they call'd out, 'Oh well! – don't it look like a bell!'
Which perplexed that Old Person of Cassel.

There was an Old Man in a barge,
Whose nose was exceedingly large;
But in fishing by night, it supported a light,
Which helped that Old Man in a barge.

There was an Old Person of Tring,
Who embellished his nose with a ring;
He gazed at the moon, every evening in June,
That ecstatic Old Person of Tring.

The Dong with a Luminous Nose

When awful darkness and silence reign
Over the great Gromboolian plain,
　　Through the long, long wintry nights; –
When the angry breakers roar
As they beat on the rocky shore; –
　　When Storm-clouds brood on the towering heights
Of the Hills of the Chankly Bore: –

Then, through the vast and gloomy dark,
There moves what seems a fiery spark,
　　A lonely spark with silvery rays
　　Piercing the coal-black night, –
　　A Meteor strange and bright: –
Hither and thither the vision strays,
　　A single lurid light.

Slowly it wanders, – pauses, – creeps, –
Anon it sparkles, – flashes and leaps;
And ever as onward it gleaming goes
A light on the Bong-tree stems it throws.
And those who watch at that midnight hour
From Hall or Terrace, or lofty Tower,
Cry, as the wild light passes along, –
　　　'The Dong! – the Dong!
　　The wandering Dong through the forest goes!
　　　The Dong! the Dong!
　　The Dong with a luminous Nose!'

Long years ago
The Dong was happy and gay,
Till he fell in love with a Jumbly Girl
Who came to those shores one day,
For the Jumblies came in a Sieve, they did, –
Landing at eve near the Zemmery Fidd
Where the Oblong Oysters grow,
And the rocks are smooth and gray.
And all the woods and the valleys rang
With the Chorus they daily and nightly sang, –
'Far and few, far and few,
Are the lands where the Jumblies live;
Their heads are green, and their hands are blue
And they went to sea in a Sieve.'

Happily, happily passed those days!
    While the cheerful Jumblies staid;
  They danced in circlets all night long,
  To the plaintive pipe of the lively Dong,
    In moonlight, shine, or shade.
For day and night he was always there
By the side of the Jumbly Girl so fair,
With her sky-blue hands, and her sea-green hair.
Till the morning came of that hateful day
When the Jumblies sailed in their Sieve away,
And the Dong was left on the cruel shore
Gazing – gazing for evermore, –
Ever keeping his weary eyes on
That pea-green sail on the far horizon, –
Singing the Jumbly Chorus still
As he sate all day on the grassy hill, –
    'Far and few, far and few,
    Are the lands where the Jumblies live;
    Their heads are green, and their hands are blue,
    And they went to sea in a Sieve.'

But when the sun was low in the West,
　　The Dong arose and said; –
– 'What little sense I once possessed
　　Has quite gone out of my head!' –
And since that day he wanders still
By lake and forest, marsh and hill,
Singing – 'O somewhere, in valley or plain
Might I find my Jumbly Girl again!
For ever I'll seek by lake and shore
Till I find my Jumbly Girl once more!'

Playing a pipe with silvery squeaks,
Since then his Jumbly Girl he seeks,
And because by night he could not see,
He gathered the bark of the Twangum Tree
　　On the flowery plain that grows.
　　And he wove him a wondrous Nose, –
A Nose as strange as a Nose could be!
Of vast proportions and painted red,
And tied with cords to the back of his head.
　　　　– In a hollow rounded space it ended
　　　　With a luminous Lamp within suspended,
　　　　　All fenced about
　　　　　With a bandage stout
　　　　　To prevent the wind from blowing it out; –
　　　　And with holes all round to send the light,
　　　　In gleaming rays on the dismal night.

And now each night, and all night long,
Over those plains still roams the Dong;
And above the wail of the Chimp and Snipe
You may hear the squeak of his plaintive pipe
While ever he seeks, but seeks in vain
To meet with his Jumbly Girl again;
Lonely and wild – all night he goes, –
The Dong with a luminous Nose!
And all who watch at the midnight hour,
From Hall or Terrace, or lofty Tower,
Cry, as they trace the Meteor bright,
Moving along through the dreary night, –
      'This is the hour when forth he goes,
      The Dong with a luminous Nose!
      Yonder – over the plain he goes;
          He goes!
          He goes;
      The Dong with a luminous Nose!'

The Pobble who has no Toes

The Pobble who has no toes
    Had once as many as we;
When they said, 'Some day you may lose them all;' –
    He replied, – 'Fish fiddle de-dee!'
And his Aunt Jobiska made him drink,
Lavender water tinged with pink,
For she said, 'The World in general knows
There's nothing so good for a Pobble's toes!'

The Pobble who has no toes,
    Swam across the Bristol Channel;
But before he set out he wrapped his nose,
    In a piece of scarlet flannel.
For his Aunt Jobiska said, 'No harm
Can come to his toes if his nose is warm;
And it's perfectly known that a Pobble's toes
Are safe, – provided he minds his nose.'

The Pobble swam fast and well
    And when boats or ships came near him
He tinkledy-binkledy-winkled a bell
    So that all the world could hear him.
And all the Sailors and Admirals cried,
When they saw him nearing the further side, –
'He has gone to fish, for his Aunt Jobiska's
Runcible Cat with crimson whiskers!'

But before he touched the shore,
   The shore of the Bristol Channel,
A sea-green Porpoise carried away
   His wrapper of scarlet flannel.
And when he came to observe his feet
Formerly garnished with toes so neat
His face at once became forlorn
On perceiving that all his toes were gone!

And nobody ever knew
   From that dark day to the present,
Whoso had taken the Pobble's toes,
   In a manner so far from pleasant.
Whether the shrimps or crawfish gray,
Or crafty Mermaids stole them away –
Nobody knew; and nobody knows
How the Pobble was robbed of his twice five toes!

The Pobble who has no toes
    Was placed in a friendly Bark,
And they rowed him back, and carried him up,
    To his Aunt Jobiska's Park.
And she made him a feast at his earnest wish
Of eggs and buttercups fried with fish; –
And she said, – 'It's a fact the whole world knows,
That Pobbles are happier without their toes.'

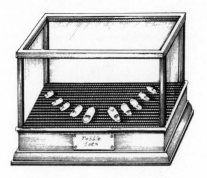

The Pobble who has no Toes (alternative version)

The Pobble went gaily on,
To a rock by the edge of the water,
And there, a-eating of crumbs and cream,
Sat King Jampoodle's daughter.
Her cap was a root of Beetroot red
With a hole cut out to insert her head;
Her gloves were yellow; her shoes were pink;
Her frock was green: and her name was Bink.

Said the Pobble – 'O Princess Bink,
A-eating of crumbs and cream!
Your beautiful face has filled my heart
With the most profound esteem!
And my Aunt Jobiska says, Man's life
Ain't worth a penny without a wife,
Whereby it will give me the greatest pleasure
If you'll marry me now, or when you've leisure!'

Said the Princess Bink – 'O! Yes!
I will certainly cross the channel
And marry you then if you'll give me now
That lovely scarlet flannel!
And besides that flannel about your nose
I trust you will give me all your toes,
To place in my Pa's Museum collection,
As proofs of your deep genteel affection!'

The Pobble unwrapped his nose,
And gave her the flannel so red,
Which, throwing her beetroot cap away,
She wreathed around her head.
And one by one he unscrewed his toes,
Which were made of the beautiful wood that grows
In his Aunt Jobiska's roorial park,
When the days are short and the nights are dark.

Said the Princess – 'O Pobble! My Pobble!
I'm yours for ever and ever!
I never will leave you my Pobble! My Pobble!
Never, and never, and never!'
Said the Pobble – 'My Binky! O bless your heart! –
– But say – would you like at once to start
Without taking leave of your dumpetty Father
Jampoodle the King?' – Said the Princess – 'Rather!'

They crossed the Channel at once
And when boats and ships came near them,
They winkelty-binkelty-tinkled their bell
So that all the world could hear them.
And all the Sailors and Admirals cried
When they saw them swim to the farther side –
'There are no more fish for his Aunt Jobiska's
Runcible Cat with crimson whiskers!'

They danced about all day,
All over the hills and dales;
They danced in every village and town
In the North and the South of Wales.
And their Aunt Jobiska made them a dish
Of Mice and Buttercups fried with fish,
For she said – 'The World in general knows
Pobbles are happier without their toes!'

There was an Old Man with a beard,
Who sat on a horse when he reared;
But they said, 'Never mind! You will fall off behind,
You propitious Old Man with a beard!'

There was an Old Person of Basing,
Whose presence of mind was amazing;
He purchased a steed, which he rode at full speed,
And escaped from the people of Basing.

There was an Old Man with a beard,
Who said, 'It is just as I feared! –
Two Owls and a Hen, four Larks and a Wren,
Have all built their nests in my beard!'

There was an Old Man in a tree,
Whose whiskers were lovely to see;
But the birds of the air, pluck'd them perfectly bare,
To make themselves nests in that tree.

27

There was an Old Man of Dundee,
Who frequented the top of a tree;
When disturbed by the crows, he abruptly arose,
And exclaimed, 'I'll return to Dundee.'

There was an Old Man in a tree,
Who was horribly bored by a Bee;
When they said, 'Does it buzz?' he replied, 'Yes, it does!
It's a regular brute of a Bee!'

There was an Old Man of Aôsta,
Who possessed a large Cow, but he lost her;
But they said, 'Don't you see, she has rushed up a tree?
You invidious Old Man of Aôsta!'

There was a Young Lady of Lucca,
Whose lovers completely forsook her;
She ran up a tree, and said, 'Fiddle-de-dee!'
Which embarrassed the people of Lucca.

There was an Old Person of Philæ,
Whose conduct was scroobious and wily;
He rushed up a Palm, when the weather was calm,
And observed all the ruins of Philæ.

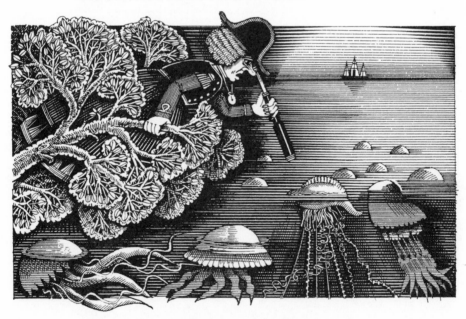

There was a Young Lady of Portugal,
Whose ideas were excessively nautical:
She climbed up a tree, to examine the sea,
But declared she would never leave Portugal.

There was an Old Lady whose folly,
Induced her to sit in a holly;
Whereon by a thorn, her dress being torn,
She quickly became melancholy.

There was a Young Lady of Firle,
Whose hair was addicted to curl;
It curled up a tree, and all over the sea,
That expansive Young Lady of Firle.

31

The Quangle Wangle's Hat

On the top of the Crumpetty Tree
   The Quangle Wangle sat,
But his face you could not see,
   On account of his Beaver Hat.
For his Hat was a hundred and two feet wide,
With ribbons and bibbons on every side
And bells, and buttons, and loops, and lace,
So that nobody ever could see the face
     Of the Quangle Wangle Quee.

The Quangle Wangle said
   To himself on the Crumpetty Tree, –
'Jam; and jelly; and bread;
   Are the best food for me!
But the longer I live on this Crumpetty Tree
The plainer than ever it seems to me
That very few people come this way
And that life on the whole is far from gay!'
     Said the Quangle Wangle Quee.

But there came to the Crumpetty Tree,
   Mr and Mrs Canary;
And they said, – 'Did you ever see
   Any spot so charmingly airy?
May we build a nest on your lovely Hat?
Mr Quangle Wangle, grant us that!
O please let us come and build a nest
Of whatever material suits you best,
     Mr Quangle Wangle Quee!'

And besides, to the Crumpetty Tree
   Came the Stork, the Duck, and the Owl;
   The Snail, and the Bumble-Bee,
   The Frog, and the Fimble Fowl;
(The Fimble Fowl, with a Corkscrew leg;)
And all of them said, – 'We humbly beg,
We may build our homes on your lovely Hat, –
Mr Quangle Wangle, grant us that!
     Mr Quangle Wangle Quee!'

And the Golden Grouse came there,
    And the Pobble who has no toes, –
And the small Olympian bear, –
    And the Dong with a luminous Nose.
And the Blue Baboon, who played the Flute, –
And the Orient Calf from the Land of Tute, –
And the Attery Squash, and the Bisky Bat, –
All came and built on the lovely Hat
        Of the Quangle Wangle Quee.

And the Quangle Wangle said
    To himself on the Crumpetty Tree, –
'When all these creatures move
    What a wonderful noise there'll be!'
And at night by the light of the Mulberry moon
They danced to the Flute of the Blue Baboon,
On the broad green leaves of the Crumpetty Tree,
And all were as happy as happy could be,
        With the Quangle Wangle Quee.

There was an Old Person of Slough,
Who danced at the end of a bough;
But they said, 'If you sneeze, you might damage the trees,
You imprudent Old Person of Slough.'

There was an Old Man of Whitehaven,
Who danced a quadrille with a Raven;
But they said, 'It's absurd, to encourage this bird!'
So they smashed that Old Man of Whitehaven.

36

There was an Old Man on the Border,
Who lived in the utmost disorder;
He danced with the cat, and made tea in his hat,
Which vexed all the folks on the Border.

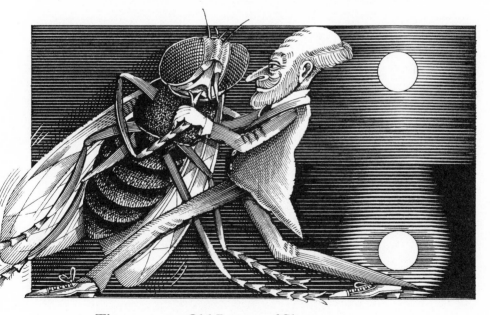

There was an Old Person of Skye,
Who waltz'd with a Bluebottle fly:
They buzz'd a sweet tune, to the light of the moon,
And entranced all the people of Skye.

There was an Old Lady of France,
Who taught little ducklings to dance;
When she said, 'Tick-a-tack!' – they only said, 'Quack!'
Which grieved that Old Lady of France.

There was an Old Man of Carlisle,
Who was left on a desolate isle:
Where he fed upon cakes, and lived wholly with snakes,
Who danced with that man of Carlisle.

There was an Old Person of Filey,
Of whom his acquaintance spoke highly;
He danced perfectly well, to the sound of a bell,
And delighted the people of Filey.

There was an Old Person of Ischia,
Whose conduct grew friskier and friskier;
He danced hornpipes and jigs, and ate thousands of figs,
That lively Old Person of Ischia.

The Akond of Swat

THE EFFECTIVE WAY TO READ THIS POEM IS TO 'GO QUICKLY
THROUGH THE TWO VERSE LINES', AND THEN 'A SHOUTING CHORUS'
SHOULD 'MAKE A LOUD AND POSITIVE STRETCH ON THE
MONOSYLLABLE HOT, TROT, ETC., ETC.'

Who, or why, or which, or *what*, Is the Akond of SWAT?
Is he tall or short, or dark or fair?
Does he sit on a stool or a sofa or chair,   or SQUAT,
       The Akond of Swat?

Is he wise or foolish, young or old?
Does he drink his soup and his coffee cold,   or HOT,
       The Akond of Swat?

Does he sing or whistle, jabber or talk,
And when riding abroad does he gallop or walk,   or TROT,
       The Akond of Swat?

Does he wear a turban, a fez, or a hat?
Does he sleep on a mattress, a bed, or a mat,   or a COT,
       The Akond of Swat?

When he writes a copy in round-hand size,
Does he cross his T's and finish his I's   with a DOT,
       The Akond of Swat?

Can he write a letter concisely clear
Without a speck or a smudge or smear   or BLOT,
       The Akond of Swat?

Do his people like him extremely well?
Or do they, whenever they can, rebel,   or PLOT,
       At the Akond of Swat?

If he catches them then, either old or young,
Does he have them chopped in pieces or hung,   or SHOT,
       The Akond of Swat?

Do his people prig in the lanes or park?
Or even at times, when days are dark,   GAROTTE?
       O the Akond of Swat!

Does he study the wants of his own dominion?
Or doesn't he care for public opinion   a JOT,
                              The Akond of Swat?

To amuse his mind do his people show him
Pictures, or anyone's last new poem,   or WHAT,
                        For the Akond of Swat?

At night if he suddenly screams and wakes,
Do they bring him only a few small cakes,   or a LOT,
                        For the Akond of Swat?

Does he live on turnips, tea, or tripe?
Does he like his shawl to be marked with a stripe,   or a DOT,
                              The Akond of Swat?

Does he like to lie on his back in a boat
Like the lady who lived in that isle remote,   SHALOTT,
                              The Akond of Swat?

Is he quiet, or always making a fuss?
Is his steward a Swiss or a Swede or a Russ,   or a SCOT,
                              The Akond of Swat?

Does he like to sit by the calm blue wave?
Or to sleep and snore in a dark green cave,   or a GROTT,
                              The Akond of Swat?

Does he drink small beer from a silver jug?
Or a bowl? Or a glass? Or a cup? Or a mug?   or a POT,
                              The Akond of Swat?

Does he beat his wife with a gold-topped pipe,
When she let the gooseberries grow too ripe,   or ROT,
                              The Akond of Swat?

Does he wear a white tie when he dines with friends,
And tie it neat in a bow with ends,   or a KNOT,
                              The Akond of Swat?

Does he like new cream, and hate mince-pies?
When he looks at the sun does he wink his eyes,   or NOT,
                              The Akond of Swat?

Does he teach his subjects to roast and bake?
Does he sail about on an inland lake,   in a YACHT,
                              The Akond of Swat?

Someone, or nobody, knows I wot
Who or which or why or what

                              Is the Akond of Swat!   41

There was an Old Man of Girgenti,
Who lived in profusion and plenty;
He lay on two chairs, and ate thousands of pears,
That susceptible man of Girgenti.

There was an Old Person whose habits,
Induced him to feed upon Rabbits;
When he'd eaten eighteen, he turned perfectly green,
Upon which he relinquished those habits.

There was an Old Person of Chili,
Whose conduct was painful and silly,
He sate on the stairs, eating apples and pears,
That imprudent Old Person of Chili.

There was an Old Person of Leeds,
Whose head was infested with beads;
She sat on a stool, and ate gooseberry fool,
Which agreed with that person of Leeds.

There was an Old Person of Leith,
Who had the most dolorous teeth;
So she had a new set. 'I'll eat quantities yet,'
Said that fortunate woman of Leith.

There was an Old Man of Calcutta,
Who perpetually ate bread and butter;
Till a great bit of muffin, on which he was stuffing,
Choked that horrid Old Man of Calcutta.

There was an Old Man of the South,
Who had an immoderate mouth;
But in swallowing a dish, that was quite full of fish,
He was choked, that Old Man of the South.

There was an Old Person of Florence,
Who held mutton chops in abhorrence;
He purchased a Bustard, and fried him in Mustard,
Which choked that Old Person of Florence.

There was an Old Man of Orleans,
Who was given to eating of beans,
Till once out of sport, he swallowed a quart,
That dyspeptic Old Man of Orleans.

There was an Old Person of Hurst,
Who drank when he was not athirst;
When they said, 'You'll grow fatter,' he answered, 'What matter?'
46   That globular person of Hurst.

There was an Old Man who said, 'Hush!
I perceive a young bird in this bush!'
When they said, 'Is it small?' he replied – 'Not at all!
It is four times as big as the bush!'

47

There was an Old Man of the Dee,
Who always was partial to tea.
Buttered toast he abhorred, and by muffins was bored,
That uncommon Old Man of the Dee.

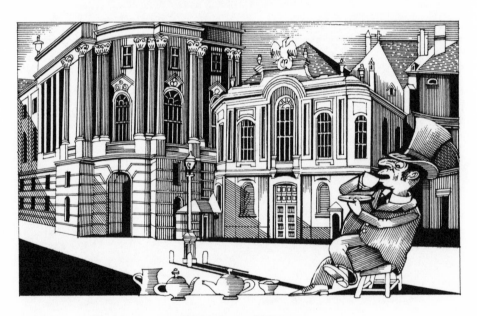

There was an Old Man of Vienna,
Who lived upon Tincture of Senna;
When that did not agree, he took Camomile Tea,
That nasty Old Man of Vienna.

There was a Young Lady of Poole,
Whose soup was excessively cool;
So she put it to boil by the aid of some oil,
That ingenious Young Lady of Poole.

There was a Young Person in pink,
Who called out for something to drink;
But they said, 'O my daughter, there's nothing but water!'
Which vexed that Young Person in pink.

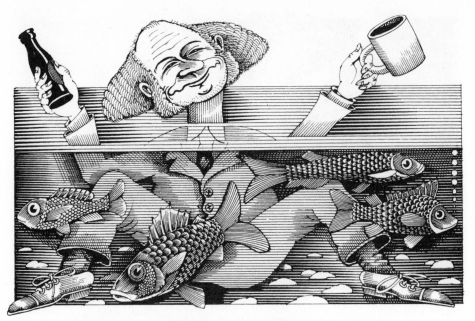

There was an Old Person of Sheen,
Whose expression was calm and serene;
He sate in the water, and drank bottled porter,
That placid Old Person of Sheen.

There was an Old Person of Troy,
Whose drink was warm brandy and soy;
Which he took with a spoon, by the light of the moon,
In sight of the city of Troy.

There was an Old Man of Columbia,
Who was thirsty, and called out for some beer;
But they brought it quite hot, in a small copper pot,
Which disgusted that man of Columbia.

There was an Old Man with an owl,
Who continued to bother and howl;
He sate on a rail, and imbibed bitter ale,
Which refreshed that Old Man and his owl.

There was an Old Person of Crowle,
Who lived in the nest of an owl;
When they screamed in the nest, he screamed out with the rest,
That depressing Old Person of Crowle.

There was a Young Lady of Russia,
Who screamed so that no one could hush her;
Her screams were extreme, no one heard such a scream,
As was screamed by that lady of Russia.

There was an Old Man who screamed out
Whenever they knocked him about;
So they took off his boots, and fed him with fruits,
And continued to knock him about.

There was an Old Man of Ibreem,
Who suddenly threaten'd to scream:
But they said, 'If you do, we will thump you quite blue,
You disgusting Old Man of Ibreem!'

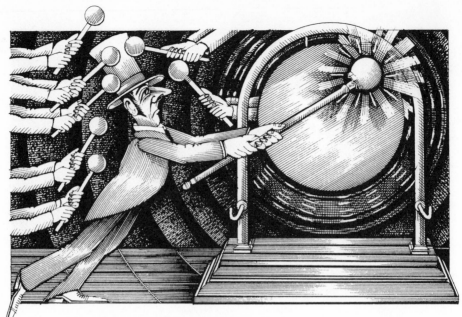

There was an Old Man with a gong,
Who bumped at it all the day long;
But they called out, 'O law! You're a horrid old bore!'
So they smashed that Old Man with a gong.

There was an Old Man of Madras,
Who rode on a cream-coloured ass;
But the length of its ears, so promoted his fears,
That it killed that Old Man of Madras.

There was a Young Person of Kew,
Whose virtues and vices were few;
But with blameable haste, she devoured some hot paste,
Which destroyed that Young Person of Kew.

There was an Old Person of Ems,
Who casually fell in the Thames;
And when he was found, they said he was drowned,
That unlucky Old Person of Ems.

There was an Old Person of Buda,
Whose conduct grew ruder and ruder;
Till at last, with a hammer, they silenced his clamour,
By smashing that person of Buda.

There was an Old Person of Cadiz,
Who was always polite to all ladies;
But in handing his daughter, he fell into the water,
Which drowned that Old Person of Cadiz.

There was an Old Man of Peru,
Who watched his wife making a stew;
But once by mistake, in a stove she did bake,
That unfortunate man of Peru.

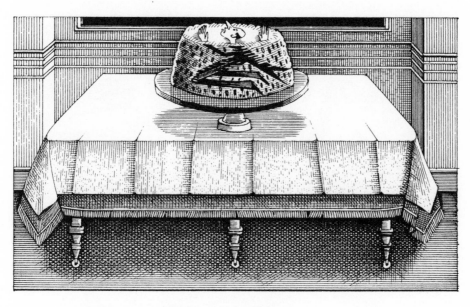

There was an Old Man of Berlin,
Whose form was uncommonly thin;
Till he once, by mistake, was mixed up in a cake,
So they baked that Old Man of Berlin.

There was a Young Man in Iowa
Who exclaimed, 'Where on earth shall I stow her!'
Of his sister he spoke, who was felled by an Oak
Which abound in the plains of Iowa.

There was a Young Lady of Norway,
Who casually sat in a doorway;
When the door squeezed her flat, she exclaimed 'What of that?'
This courageous Young Lady of Norway.

There was an Old Person of Pinner,
As thin as a lath, if not thinner;
They dressed him in white, and roll'd him up tight,
That elastic Old Person of Pinner.

There was an Old Man of Cashmere,
Whose movements were scroobious and queer;
Being slender and tall, he looked over a wall,
And perceived two fat ducks of Cashmere.

There was an Old Man of Spithead,
Who opened the window, and said,
'Fil-jomble, fil-jumble, fil-rumble-come-tumble!'
That doubtful Old Man of Spithead.

There was an Old Man at a casement,
Who held up his hands in amazement;
When they said, 'Sir! You'll fall!' he replied, 'Not at all!'
That incipient Old Man at a casement.

There was an Old Person of Rimini,
Who said, 'Gracious! Goodness! O Gimini!'
When they said, 'Please be still!' she ran down a hill,
And was never more heard of at Rimini.

There was an Old Person of Wick,
Who said, 'Tick-a-Tick, Tick-a-Tick;
Chickabee, Chickabaw,' and he said nothing more,
That laconic Old Person of Wick.

There was a Young Lady in blue,
Who said, 'Is it you? Is it you?'
When they said, 'Yes, it is,' – she replied only, 'Whizz!'
That ungracious Young Lady in blue.

There was a Young Lady of Parma,
Whose conduct grew calmer and calmer;
When they said, 'Are you dumb?' she merely said, 'Hum!'
That provoking Young Lady of Parma.

There was an Old Person of Sestri,
Who sate himself down in the vestry,
When they said, 'You are wrong!' – he merely said, 'Bong!'
That repulsive Old Person of Sestri.

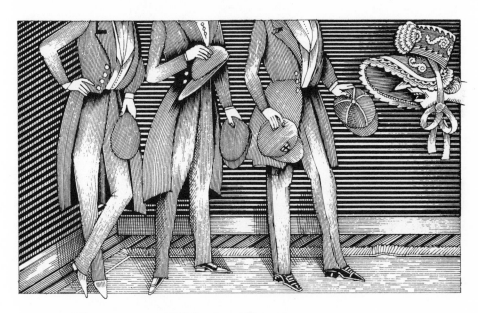

There was an Old Lady of Prague,
Whose language was horribly vague.
When they said, 'Are these caps?' she answered, 'Perhaps!'
That oracular lady of Prague.

There was an Old Man in a garden,
Who always begged everyone's pardon;
When they asked him, 'What for?' – he replied, 'You're a bore!
And I trust you'll go out of my garden.'

There was an Old Man who forgot,
That his tea was excessively hot.
When they said, 'Let it cool,' he answered, 'You fool!
I shall pour it back into the pot.'

There was an Old Man with a poker,
Who painted his face with red ochre;
When they said, 'You're a Guy!' he made no reply,
But knocked them all down with his poker.

There was an Old Person of Minety
Who purchased five hundred and ninety
Large apples and pears, which he threw unawares,
At the heads of the people of Minety.

There was an Old Person of Newry,
Whose manners were tinctured with fury;
He tore all the rugs, and broke all the jugs
Within twenty miles' distance of Newry.

There was an Old Person of Bangor,
Whose face was distorted with anger,
He tore off his boots, and subsisted on roots,
That borascible person of Bangor.

There was an Old Person of Stroud,
Who was horribly jammed in a crowd;
Some she slew with a kick, some she scrunched with a stick,
That impulsive Old Person of Stroud.

There was an Old Person of Sark,
Who made an unpleasant remark;
But they said, 'Don't you see what a brute you must be!
You obnoxious Old Person of Sark.'

There was an Old Lady of Chertsey,
Who made a remarkable curtsey;
She twirled round and round, till she sunk underground,
Which distressed all the people of Chertsey.

There was an Old Man of the West,
Who never could get any rest;
So they set him to spin, on his nose and his chin,
Which cured that Old Man of the West.

There was an Old Person of Anerley,
Whose conduct was strange and unmannerly;
He rushed down the Strand, with a Pig in each hand,
But returned in the evening to Anerley.

There was an Old Person of Burton,
Whose answers were rather uncertain;
When they said, 'How d'ye do?' he replied, 'Who are you?'
That distressing Old Person of Burton.

There was an Old Man of Moldavia,
Who had the most curious behaviour;
For while he was able, he slept on a table.
That funny Old Man of Moldavia.

There was an Old Person of Spain,
Who hated all trouble and pain;
So he sate on a chair, with his feet in the air,
That umbrageous Old Person of Spain.

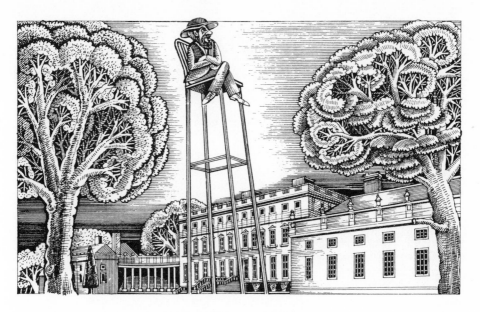

There was an Old Man of Kildare,
Who climbed into a very high chair;
When he said, – 'Here I stays, till the end of my days',
That immovable man of Kildare.

There was an Old Man of the Coast,
Who placidly sat on a post;
But when it was cold, he relinquished his hold,
And called for some hot buttered toast.

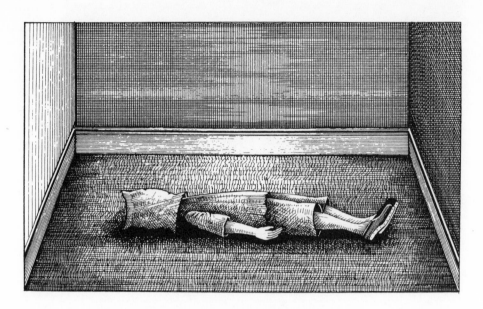

There was an Old Man of Hong Kong,
Who never did anything wrong;
He lay on his back, with his head in a sack,
That innocuous Old Man of Hong Kong.

There was an Old Man of Port Grigor,
Whose actions were noted for vigour;
He stood on his head, till his waistcoat turned red,
That eclectic Old Man of Port Grigor.

There was an Old Lady of Winchelsea,
Who said, 'If you needle or pin shall see,
On the floor of my room, sweep it up with the broom!'
That exhaustive Old Lady of Winchelsea!

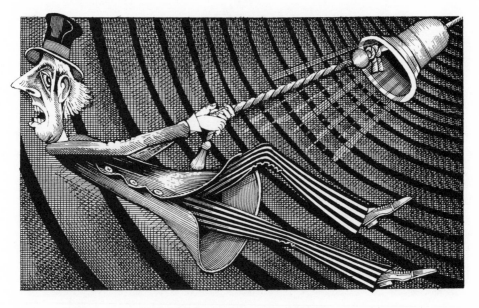

There was an Old Man who said, 'Well!
Will *nobody* answer this bell?
I have pulled day and night, till my hair has grown white,
But nobody answers this bell!'

There was an Old Man of th' Abruzzi,
So blind that he couldn't his foot see;
When they said, 'That's your toe,' he replied, 'Is it so?'
That doubtful Old Man of th' Abruzzi.

There was a Young Lady whose eyes,
Were unique as to colour and size;
When she opened them wide, people all turned aside,
And started away in surprise.

There was an Old Person of Down,
Whose face was adorned with a frown;
When he opened the door, for one minute or more,
He alarmed all the people of Down.

There was an Old Man of the Isles,
Whose face was pervaded with smiles:
He sung high dum diddle, and played on the fiddle,
That amiable man of the Isles.

There was an Old Person of Blythe,
Who cut up his meat with a scythe;
When they said, 'Well! I never!' – he cried, 'Scythes for ever!'
That lively Old Person of Blythe.

There was an Old Person of Diss,
Who said, 'It is this! It is this!'
When they said, 'What?' or 'Which?' – he jumped into a ditch,
Which absorbed that Old Person of Diss.

There was an Old Man, who when little
Fell casually into a kettle;
But, growing too stout, he could never get out,
So he passed all his life in that kettle.

There was an Old Person of Bar,
Who passed all her life in a jar,
Which she painted pea-green, to appear more serene,
That placid Old Person of Bar.

Mr and Mrs Discobbolos

Mr and Mrs Discobbolos
    Climbed to the top of a wall.
    And they sate to watch the sunset sky
    And to hear the Nupiter Piffkin cry
    And the Biscuit Buffalo call.
They took up a roll and some Camomile tea,
And both were as happy as happy could be –
    Till Mrs Discobbolos said, –
    'Oh! W! X! Y! Z!
    It has just come into my head –
Suppose we should happen to fall!!!!!
          Darling Mr Discobbolos

'Suppose we should fall down flumpetty
        Just like pieces of stone!
    On to the thorns, – or into the moat!
    What would become of your new green coat
        And might you not break a bone?
It never occurred to me before –
That perhaps we shall never go down any more!'
            And Mrs Discobbolos said –
            'Oh! W! X! Y! Z!
        What put it into your head
    To climb up this wall? – my own
                Darling Mr Discobbolos?'

Mr Discobbolos answered, –
        'At first it gave me pain, –
    And I felt my ears turn perfectly pink
    When your exclamation made me think
        We might never get down again!
But now I believe it is wiser far
To remain for ever just where we are.' –
            And Mr Discobbolos said,
                'Oh! W! X! Y! Z!
            It has just come into my head –
    – We shall never go down again –
                Dearest Mrs Discobbolos!'

So Mr and Mrs Discobbolos
        Stood up, and began to sing,
    'Far away from hurry and strife
Here we will pass the rest of life,
        Ding a dong, ding dong, ding!
We want no knives nor forks nor chairs,
No tables nor carpets nor household cares,
            From worry of life we've fled –
            Oh! W! X! Y! Z!
            There is no more trouble ahead,
    Sorrow or any such thing –
                For Mr and Mrs Discobbolos!'   79

Mr and Mrs Discobbolos SECOND PART

Mr and Mrs Discobbolos
    Lived on top of the wall,
  For twenty years, a month and a day,
  Till their hair had grown all pearly gray,
  And their teeth began to fall.
They never were ill, or at all dejected,
By all admired, and by some respected,
    Till Mrs Discobbolos said,
    'O, W! X! Y! Z!
    It has just come into my head,
We have no more room at all –
                Darling Mr Discobbolos!

'Look at our six fine boys!
  And our six sweet girls so fair!
Upon this wall they have all been born,
And not one of the twelve has happened to fall
  Through my maternal care!
Surely they should not pass their lives
Without any chance of husbands or wives!'
    And Mrs Discobbolos said,
    'O, W! X! Y! Z!
    Did it never come into your head
That our lives must be lived elsewhere,
                Dearest Mr Discobbolos?

'They have never been at a ball,
  Nor have even seen a bazaar!
Nor have heard folks say in a tone all hearty
"What loves of girls" (at a garden party)
  "Those Misses Discobbolos are!"
Morning and night it drives me wild
To think of the fate of each darling child!'
    But Mr Discobbolos said,
    'O, W! X! Y! Z!
    What has come to your fiddledum head!
What a runcible goose you are!
                Octopod Mrs Discobbolos!'

Suddenly Mr Discobbolos
      Slid from the top of the wall;
   And beneath it he dug a dreadful trench,
   And filled it with dynamite, gunpowder gench,
      And aloud he began to call –
'Let the wild bee sing,
And the blue bird hum!
For the end of your lives has certainly come!'
      And Mrs Discobbolos said,
      'O, W! X! Y! Z!
      We shall presently all be dead,
   On this ancient runcible wall,
                  Terrible Mr Discobbolos!'

Pensively, Mr Discobbolos
      Sat with his back to the wall;
   He lighted a match, and fired the train,
   And the mortified mountain echoed again
      To the sound of an awful fall!
And all the Discobbolos family flew
In thousands of bits to the sky so blue,
      And no one was left to have said,
      'O, W! X! Y! Z!
      Has it come into anyone's head
   That the end has happened to all
                  Of the whole of the Clan Discobbolos?'

There was an Old Man on some rocks,
Who shut his wife up in a box,
When she said, 'Let me out,' he exclaimed, 'Without doubt,
You will pass all your life in that box.'

There was an Old Person of Harrow
Who bought a mahogany barrow,
For he said to his wife, 'You're the joy of my life!
And I'll wheel you all day in this barrow!'

There was an Old Man of Jamaica,
Who suddenly married a Quaker!
But she cried out – 'O lack! I have married a black!'
Which distressed that Old Man of Jamaica.

There was an Old Person of Hyde,
Who walked by the shore with his bride,
Till a Crab who came near, fill'd their bosoms with fear,
And they said, 'Would we'd never left Hyde!'

Mr and Mrs Spikky Sparrow

On a little piece of wood,
Mr Spikky Sparrow stood;
Mrs Sparrow sate close by,
A-making of an insect pie,
For her little children five,
In the nest and all alive,
Singing with a cheerful smile
To amuse them all the while

Twikky wikky wikky wee,
Wikky bikky twikky tee,
    Spikky bikky bee!

Mrs Spikky Sparrow said,
'Spikky, Darling! In my head
Many thoughts of trouble come,
Like to flies upon a plum!
All last night, among the trees,
I heard you cough, I heard you sneeze;
And, thought I, it's come to that
Because he does not wear a hat!
    Chippy wippy sikky tee!
    Bikky wikky tikky mee!
    Spikky chippy wee!

'Not that you are growing old,
But the nights are growing cold.
No one stays out all night long
Without a hat: I'm sure it's wrong!'
Mr Spikky said, 'How kind,
Dear! you are, to speak your mind!
All your life I wish you luck!
You are! you are! a lovely duck!
    Witchy witchy witchy wee!
    Twitchy witchy witchy bee!
    Tikky tikky tee!

'I was also sad, and thinking,
When one day I saw you winking,
And I heard you sniffle-snuffle,
And I saw your feathers ruffle;
To myself I sadly said,
She's neuralgia in her head!
That dear head has nothing on it!
Ought she not to wear a bonnet?
    Witchy kitchy kitchy wee?
    Spikky wikky mikky bee?
    Chippy wippy chee?

'Let us both fly up to town!
There I'll buy you such a gown!
Which, completely in the fashion,
You shall tie a sky-blue sash on.
And a pair of slippers neat,
To fit your darling little feet,
So that you will look and feel
Quite galloobious and genteel!
    Jikky wikky bikky see,
        Chicky bikky wikky bee,
            Twicky witchy wee!'

So they both to London went,
Alighting on the Monument,
Whence they flew down swiftly – pop,
Into Moses' wholesale shop;
There they bought a hat and bonnet,
And a gown with spots upon it,
A satin sash of Cloxam blue,
And a pair of slippers too.
    Zikky wikky mikky bee,
        Witchy witchy mitchy kee,
            Sikky tikky wee.

Then when so completely drest,
Back they flew, and reached their nest.
Their children cried, 'O Ma and Pa!
How truly beautiful you are!'
Said they, 'We trust that cold or pain
We shall never feel again!
While, perched on tree, or house, or steeple,
We now shall look like other people.
    Witchy witchy witchy wee,
        Twikky mikky bikky bee,
            Zikky sikky tee.'

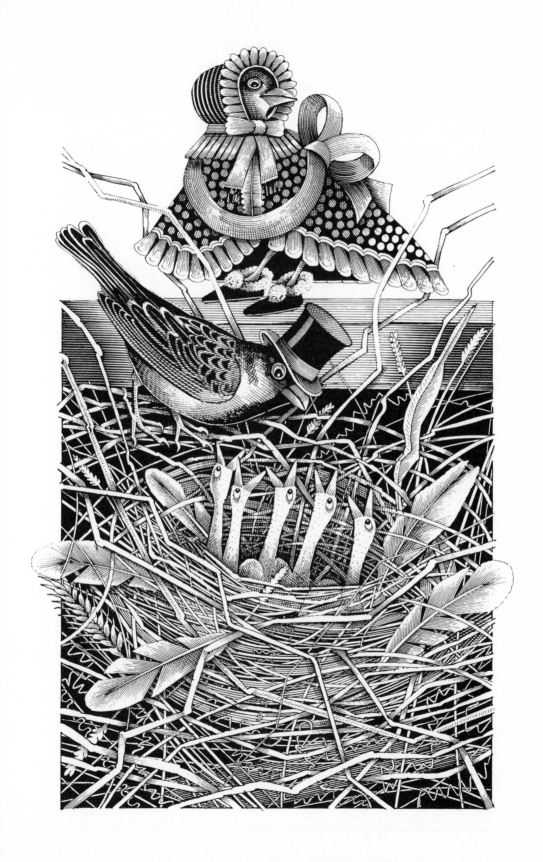

The Courtship of the Yonghy-Bonghy-Bò

On the Coast of Coromandel
Where the early pumpkins blow,
In the middle of the woods
   Lived the Yonghy-Bonghy-Bò.
Two old chairs, and half a candle, –
One old jug without a handle, –
     These were all his worldly goods:
     In the middle of the woods,
     These were all the worldly goods,
   Of the Yonghy-Bonghy-Bò,
   Of the Yonghy-Bonghy-Bò.

Once, among the Bong-trees walking
   Where the early pumpkins blow,
     To a little heap of stones
   Came the Yonghy-Bonghy-Bò.
There he heard a Lady talking,
To some milk-white Hens of Dorking, –
     ' 'Tis the Lady Jingly Jones!
     On that little heap of stones
     Sits the Lady Jingly Jones!'
   Said the Yonghy-Bonghy-Bò,
   Said the Yonghy-Bonghy-Bò.

'Lady Jingly! Lady Jingly!
   Sitting where the pumpkins blow,
     Will you come and be my wife?'
   Said the Yonghy-Bonghy-Bò.
'I am tired of living singly, –
On this coast so wild and shingly, –
     I'm a-weary of my life:
     If you'll come and be my wife,
     Quite serene would be my life!' –
   Said the Yonghy-Bonghy-Bò,
   Said the Yonghy-Bonghy-Bò.

'On this Coast of Coromandel,
    Shrimps and watercresses grow,
        Prawns are plentiful and cheap,'
    Said the Yonghy-Bonghy-Bò.
'You shall have my Chairs and candle,
And my jug without a handle! –
        Gaze upon the rolling deep
        (Fish is plentiful and cheap)
        As the sea, my love is deep!'
    Said the Yonghy-Bonghy-Bò,
    Said the Yonghy-Bonghy-Bò.

Lady Jingly answered sadly,
    And her tears began to flow, –
        'Your proposal comes too late,
    Mr Yonghy-Bonghy-Bò!
I would be your wife most gladly!'
(Here she twirled her fingers madly)
        'But in England I've a mate!
        Yes! you've asked me far too late,
        For in England I've a mate,
    Mr Yonghy-Bonghy-Bò!
    Mr Yonghy-Bonghy-Bò!'

'Mr Jones – (his name is Handel, –
    Handel Jones, Esquire, & Co.)
        Dorking fowls delights to send,
    Mr Yonghy-Bonghy-Bò!
Keep, oh! keep your chairs and candle,
And your jug without a handle, –
        I can merely be your friend!
        – Should my Jones more Dorkings send,
        I will give you three, my friend!
    Mr Yonghy-Bonghy-Bò!
    Mr Yonghy-Bonghy-Bò!'

'Though you've such a tiny body,
    And your head so large doth grow, –
    Though your hat may blow away,
    Mr Yonghy-Bonghy-Bò!
Though you're such a Hoddy Doddy –
Yet I wish that I could modi-
    fy the words I needs must say!
    Will you please to go away?
    That is all I have to say –
    Mr Yonghy-Bonghy-Bò!
    Mr Yonghy-Bonghy-Bò!'

Down the slippery slopes of Myrtle,
   Where the early pumpkins blow,
      To the calm and silent sea
   Fled the Yonghy-Bonghy-Bò.
There, beyond the Bay of Gurtle,
Lay a large and lively Turtle; –
      'You're the Cove,' he said, 'for me
      On your back beyond the sea,
      Turtle, you shall carry me!'
   Said the Yonghy-Bonghy-Bò,
   Said the Yonghy-Bonghy-Bò.

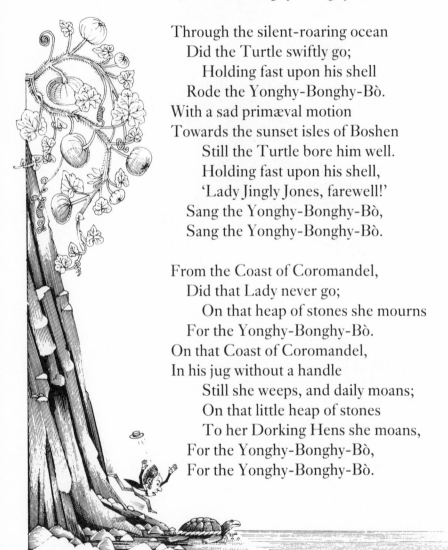

Through the silent-roaring ocean
   Did the Turtle swiftly go;
      Holding fast upon his shell
   Rode the Yonghy-Bonghy-Bò.
With a sad primæval motion
Towards the sunset isles of Boshen
      Still the Turtle bore him well.
      Holding fast upon his shell,
      'Lady Jingly Jones, farewell!'
   Sang the Yonghy-Bonghy-Bò,
   Sang the Yonghy-Bonghy-Bò.

From the Coast of Coromandel,
   Did that Lady never go;
      On that heap of stones she mourns
   For the Yonghy-Bonghy-Bò.
On that Coast of Coromandel,
In his jug without a handle
      Still she weeps, and daily moans;
      On that little heap of stones
      To her Dorking Hens she moans,
   For the Yonghy-Bonghy-Bò,
   For the Yonghy-Bonghy-Bò.

There was an Old Man of Boulak,
Who sate on a Crocodile's back;
But they said, 'Tow'rds the night, he may probably bite,
Which might vex you, Old Man of Boulak!'

There was an Old Person of Ickley,
Who could not abide to ride quickly,
He rode to Karnak, on a tortoise's back,
That moony Old Person of Ickley.

There was an Old Man of Dunluce,
Who went out to sea on a goose:
When he'd gone out a mile, he observ'd with a smile,
'It is time to return to Dunluce.'

There was an Old Man of Messina,
Whose daughter was named Opsibeena;
She wore a small wig, and rode out on a pig,
To the perfect delight of Messina.

There was an Old Person of Rye,
Who went up to town on a fly;
But they said, 'If you cough, you are safe to fall off!
You abstemious Old Person of Rye!'

There was an Old Person of Ware,
Who rode on the back of a bear:
When they ask'd, 'Does it trot?' – he said 'Certainly not!
He's a Moppsikon Floppsikon bear!'

There was an Old Man whose despair
Induced him to purchase a hare:
Whereon one fine day, he rode wholly away,
Which partly assuaged his despair.

There was an Old Person of Ealing,
Who was wholly devoid of good feeling;
He drove a small gig, with three Owls and a Pig,
Which distressed all the people of Ealing.

There was an Old Man in a boat,
Who said, 'I'm afloat! I'm afloat!'
When they said, 'No! you ain't!' he was ready to faint,
That unhappy Old Man in a boat.

There was an Old Person of Grange,
Whose manners were scroobious and strange;
He sailed to St Blubb, in a waterproof tub,
That aquatic Old Person of Grange.

There was an Old Sailor of Compton,
Whose vessel a rock it once bump'd on,
The shock was so great, that it damaged the pate,
Of that singular sailor of Compton.

The Jumblies

They went to sea in a Sieve, they did,
   In a Sieve they went to sea;
In spite of all their friends could say,
On a winter's morn, on a stormy day,
   In a Sieve they went to sea!
And when the Sieve turned round and round,
And everyone cried, 'You'll all be drowned!'
They called aloud, 'Our Sieve ain't big,
But we don't care a button! We don't care a fig!
   In a Sieve we'll go to sea!'
     Far and few, far and few,
       Are the lands where the Jumblies live;
       Their heads are green, and their hands are blue,
       And they went to sea in a Sieve.

They sailed away in a Sieve, they did,
   In a Sieve they sailed so fast,
With only a beautiful pea-green veil
Tied with a riband by way of a sail,
   To a small tobacco-pipe mast;
And everyone said, who saw them go,
'O won't they be soon upset, you know!
For the sky is dark, and the voyage is long,
And happen what may, it's extremely wrong
   In a Sieve to sail so fast!'
     Far and few, far and few,
       Are the lands where the Jumblies live;
       Their heads are green, and their hands are blue,
       And they went to sea in a Sieve.

The water it soon came in, it did,
    The water it soon came in;
So to keep them dry, they wrapped their feet
In a pinky paper all folded neat,
    And they fastened it down with a pin.
And they passed the night in a crockery-jar,
And each of them said, 'How wise we are!
Though the sky be dark, and the voyage be long,
Yet we never can think we were rash or wrong,
    While round in our Sieve we spin!'
        Far and few, far and few,
            Are the lands where the Jumblies live;
        Their heads are green, and their hands are blue,
            And they went to sea in a Sieve.

And all night long they sailed away;
    And when the sun went down,
They whistled and warbled a moony song
To the echoing sound of a coppery gong,
    In the shade of the mountains brown.
'O Timballo! How happy we are,
When we live in a sieve and a crockery-jar,
And all night long in the moonlight pale,
We sail away with a pea-green sail,
    In the shade of the mountains brown!'
        Far and few, far and few,
            Are the lands where the Jumblies live;
            Their heads are green, and their hands are blue,
                And they went to sea in a Sieve.

They sailed to the Western Sea, they did,
    To a land all covered with trees,
And they bought an Owl, and a useful Cart,
And a pound of Rice, and a Cranberry Tart,
    And a hive of silvery Bees.
And they bought a Pig, and some green Jack-daws,
And a lovely Monkey with lollipop paws,
And forty bottles of Ring-Bo-Ree,
    And no end of Stilton Cheese.
        Far and few, far and few,
            Are the lands where the Jumblies live;
            Their heads are green, and their hands are blue,
            And they went to sea in a Sieve.

And in twenty years they all came back,
   In twenty years or more,
And everyone said, 'How tall they've grown!
For they've been to the Lakes, and the Torrible Zone,
   And the hills of the Chankly Bore';
And they drank their health, and gave them a feast
Of dumplings made of beautiful yeast;
And everyone said, 'If we only live,
We too will go to sea in a Sieve, –
   To the hills of the Chankly Bore!'
      Far and few, far and few,
         Are the lands where the Jumblies live;
         Their heads are green, and their hands are blue,
            And they went to sea in a Sieve.

There was an Old Man of the North,
Who fell into a basin of broth;
But a laudable cook, fished him out with a hook,
Which saved that Old Man of the North.

There was an Old Man of Nepaul,
From his horse had a terrible fall;
But, though split quite in two, by some very strong glue,
They mended that man of Nepaul.

There was a Young Lady of Turkey,
Who wept when the weather was murky;
When the day turned out fine, she ceased to repine,
That capricious Young Lady of Turkey.

There was an Old Person of Nice,
Whose associates were usually Geese.
They walked out together, in all sorts of weather.
That affable person of Nice!

107

There was an Old Man whose remorse,
Induced him to drink Caper Sauce;
For they said, 'If mixed up, with some cold claret-cup,
It will certainly soothe your remorse!'

There was an Old Person of Pett,
Who was partly consumed by regret;
He sate in a cart, and ate cold apple tart,
Which relieved that Old Person of Pett.

There was an Old Person of Fife,
Who was greatly disgusted with life;
They sang him a ballad, and fed him on salad,
Which cured that Old Person of Fife.

There was an Old Person of Prague,
Who was suddenly seized with the plague;
But they gave him some butter, which caused him to mutter,
And cured that Old Person of Prague.

There was an Old Man whose giardino
Produced only one little bean O!
When he said – 'That's enough!' – they answered, 'What stuff!
You never can live on *one* bean O!'

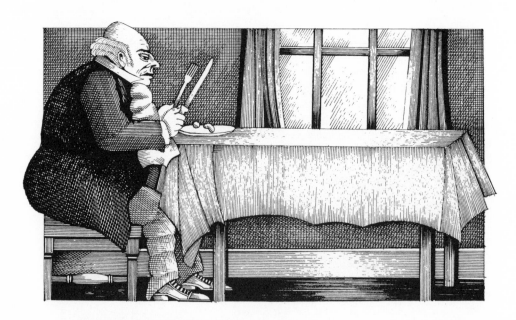

There was an Old Person of Dean
Who dined on one pea, and one bean;
For he said, 'More than that, would make me too fat,'
That cautious Old Person of Dean.

There was an Old Man of El Hums,
Who lived upon nothing but crumbs,
Which he picked off the ground, with the other birds round,
In the roads and the lanes of El Hums.

There was an Old Man of Kilkenny,
Who never had more than a penny;
He spent all that money, in onions and honey,
That wayward Old Man of Kilkenny.

There was an Old Person of Putney,
Whose food was roast spiders and chutney,
Which he took with his tea, within sight of the sea,
That romantic Old Person of Putney.

There was an Old Person of Ewell,
Who chiefly subsisted on gruel;
But to make it more nice, he inserted some mice,
Which refreshed that Old Person of Ewell.

There was an Old Person of Bromley,
Whose ways were not cheerful or comely;
He sate in the dust, eating spiders and crust,
That unpleasing Old Person of Bromley.

There was an Old Person of Brussels,
Who lived upon Brandy and Mussels.
When he rushed through the town, he knocked most
                                         people down,
Which distressed all the people of Brussels.

There was an Old Man on the Humber,
Who dined on a cake of burnt Umber;
When he said – 'It's enough!' – they only said, 'Stuff!
You amazing Old Man on the Humber!'

There was an Old Person of Rheims,
Who was troubled with horrible dreams;
So, to keep him awake, they fed him with cake,
Which amused that Old Person of Rheims.

There was an Old Man of the hills,
Who lived upon Syrup of Squills;
Which he drank all night long, to the sound of a gong,
That persistent Old Man of the hills.

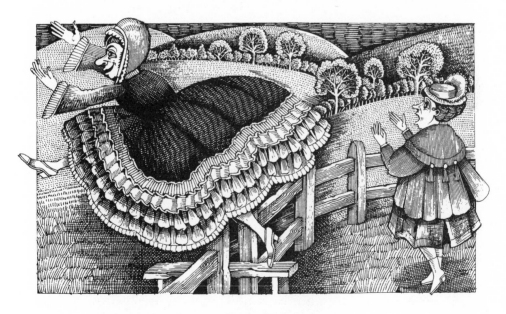

There was a Young Girl of Majorca,
Whose aunt was a very fast walker;
She walked seventy miles, and leaped fifteen stiles,
Which astonished that girl of Majorca.

The Two Old Bachelors

Two old Bachelors were living in one house;
One caught a Muffin, the other caught a Mouse.
Said he who caught the Muffin to him who caught the Mouse, –
'This happens just in time! For we've nothing in the house,
Save a tiny slice of lemon and a teaspoonful of honey,
And what to do for dinner – since we haven't any money?
And what can we expect if we haven't any dinner,
But to lose our teeth and eyelashes and keep on growing thinner?'

Said he who caught the Mouse to him who caught the Muffin, –
'We might cook this little Mouse, if we only had some Stuffin'!
If we had but Sage and Onion we could do extremely well,
But how to get that Stuffin' it is difficult to tell' –

Those two old Bachelors ran quickly to the town
And asked for Sage and Onions as they wandered up and down;
They borrowed two large Onions, but no Sage was to be found
In the Shops, or in the Market, or in all the Gardens round.

But someone said, – 'A hill there is, a little to the north,
And to its purpledicular top a narrow way leads forth; –
And there among the rugged rocks abides an ancient Sage, –
An earnest Man, who reads all day a most perplexing page.
Climb up, and seize him by the toes! – all studious as he sits, –
And pull him down, – and chop him into endless little bits!
Then mix him with your Onion (cut up likewise into Scraps) –
When your Stuffin' will be ready – and very good: perhaps.'

116

Those two old Bachelors without loss of time
The nearly purpledicular crags at once began to climb;
And at the top, among the rocks, all seated in a nook,
They saw that Sage, a-reading of a most enormous book.

'You earnest Sage!' aloud they cried, 'your book you've read enough in! –
We wish to chop you into bits to mix you into Stuffin'!' –

But that old Sage looked calmly up, and with his awful book,
At those two Bachelors' bald heads a certain aim he took; –
And over Crag and precipice they rolled promiscuous down, –
At once they rolled, and never stopped in lane or field or town, –
And when they reached their house, they found
    (besides their want of Stuffin')
The Mouse had fled; – and, previously, had eaten up the Muffin.

They left their home in silence by the once convivial door.
And from that hour those Bachelors were never heard of more.

There was an Old Person of Chester,
Whom several small children did pester;
They threw some large stones, which broke most of his bones,
And displeased that Old Person of Chester.

There was an Old Person of Bow,
Whom nobody happened to know;
So they gave him some soap, and said coldly, 'We hope
You will go back directly to Bow!'

There was an Old Man of Thermopylæ,
Who never did anything properly;
But they said, 'If you choose, to boil eggs in your shoes,
You shall never remain in Thermopylæ.'

There was an Old Person of Loo,
Who said, 'What on earth shall I do?'
When they said, 'Go away!' – she continued to stay,
That vexatious Old Person of Loo.

There was a Young Person of Janina,
Whose uncle was always a fanning her;
When he fanned off her head, she smiled sweetly, and said,
'You propitious Old Person of Janina!'

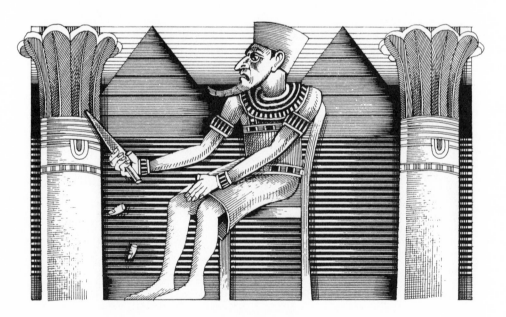

There was an Old Man of the Nile,
Who sharpened his nails with a file;
Till he cut off his thumbs, and said calmly, 'This comes –
Of sharpening one's nails with a file!'

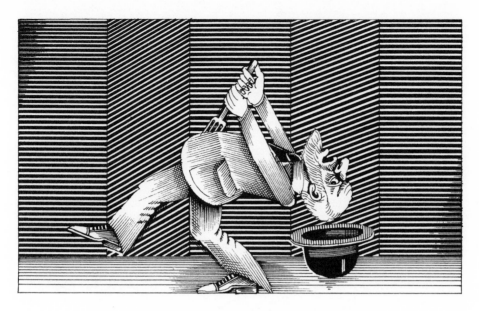

There was an Old Man of New York,
Who murdered himself with a fork;
But nobody cried, though he very soon died,
For that silly Old Man of New York.

There was an Old Person of Tartary,
Who divided his jugular artery;
But he screeched to his wife, and she said, 'Oh, my life!
Your death will be felt by all Tartary!'

There was an Old Man of Peru,
Who never knew what he should do;
So he tore off his hair, and behaved like a bear,
That intrinsic Old Man of Peru.

There was an Old Man of Corfu,
Who never knew what he should do;
So he rushed up and down, till the sun made him brown,
That bewildered Old Man of Corfu.

There was an Old Man of Cape Horn,
Who wished he had never been born;
So he sat on a chair, till he died of despair,
That dolorous man of Cape Horn.

There was a Young Lady in white,
Who looked out at the depths of the night;
But the birds of the air, filled her heart with despair,
And oppressed that Young Lady in white.

Eclogue

[*Interlocutors* – MR LEAR AND MR AND MRS SYMONDS]

Edwardus – What makes you look so black, so glum, so cross?
          Is it neuralgia, headache, or remorse?

Johannes – What makes you look as cross, or even more so?
          Less like a man than is a broken Torso?

    E. – What if my life is odious, should I grin?
          If you are savage, need I care a pin?

    J. – And if I suffer, am I then an owl?
          May I not frown and grind my teeth and growl?

    E. – Of course you may; but may not I growl too?
          May I not frown and grind my teeth like you?

    J. – See Catherine comes! To her, to her,
          Let each his several miseries refer;
          She shall decide whose woes are least or worst,
          And which, as growler, shall rank last or first.

Catherine – Proceed to growl, in silence I'll attend,
          And hear your foolish growlings to the end;
          And when they're done, I shall correctly judge
          Which of your griefs are real or only fudge.
          Begin, let each his mournful voice prepare,
          (And, pray, however angry, do not swear!)

    J. – We came abroad for warmth, and find sharp cold
          Cannes is an imposition, and we're sold.

    E. – Why did I leave my native land, to find
          Sharp hailstones, snow, and most disgusting wind?

    J. – What boots it that we orange trees or lemons see,
          If we must suffer from *such* vile inclemency?

E. – Why did I take the lodgings I have got,
Where all I don't want is: – all I want not?

J. – Last week I called aloud, O! O! O! O!
The ground is wholly overspread with snow!
Is that at any rate a theme for mirth
Which makes a sugar-cake of all the earth?

E. – Why must I sneeze and snuffle, groan and cough,
If my hat's on my head, or if it's off?
Why must I sink all poetry in this prose,
The everlasting blowing of my nose?

J. – When I walk out the mud my footsteps clogs,
Besides, I suffer from attacks of dogs.

E. – Me a vast awful bulldog, black and brown,
Completely terrified when near the town;
As calves, perceiving butchers, trembling reel,
So did *my* calves the approaching monster feel.

J. – Already from two rooms we're driven away,
Because the beastly chimneys smoke all day:
Is this a trifle, say? Is this a joke?
That we, like hams, should be becooked in smoke?

E. – Say! What avails it that my servant speaks
Italian, English, Arabic, and Greek,
Besides Albanian: if he don't speak French,
How can he ask for salt, or shrimps, or tench?

J. – When on the foolish hearth fresh wood I place,
It whistles, sings, and squeaks, before my face:
And if it does unless the fire burns bright,
And if it does, yet squeaks, how can I write?

E. – Alas! I needs must go and call on swells,
That they may say, 'Pray draw me the Estrelles.'
On one I went last week to leave a card,   127

The swell was out – the servant eyed me hard:
'This chap's a thief disguised,' his face expressed:
If I go there again, may I be blest!

J. – Why must I suffer in this wind and gloom?
Roomattics in a vile cold attic room?

E. – Swells drive about the road with haste and fury,
As Jehu drove about all over Jewry.
Just now, while walking slowly, I was all but
Run over by the Lady Emma Talbot,
Whom not long since a lovely babe I knew,
With eyes and cap-ribbons of perfect blue.

J. – Downstairs and upstairs, every blessed minute,
There's each room with pianofortes in it.
How can I write with noises such as those?
And, being always discomposed, compose?

E. – Seven Germans through my garden lately strayed,
And all on instruments of torture played;
They blew, they screamed, they yelled: how can I paint
Unless my room is quiet, which it ain't?

J. – How can I study if a hundred flies
Each moment blunder into both my eyes?

E. – How can I draw with green or blue or red,
If flies and beetles vex my old bald head?

J. – How can I translate German Metaphys-
Ics, if mosquitoes round my forehead whizz?

E. – I've bought some bacon (though it's much too fat)
But round the house there prowls a hideous cat:
Once should I see my bacon in her mouth,
What care I if my rooms look north or south?

J. – Pain from a pane in one cracked window comes,
Which sings and whistles, buzzes, shrieks and hums;

In vain amain with pain the pane with this chord
I fain would strain to stop the beastly *dis*cord!

E. – If rain and wind and snow and such like ills
        Continue here, how shall I pay my bills?
        For who through cold and slush and rain will come
        To see my drawings and to purchase some?
        And if they don't, what destiny is mine?
        How can I ever get to Palestine?

J. – The blinding sun strikes through the olive trees,
        When I walk out, and always makes me sneeze.

E. – Next door, if all night long the moon is shining,
        There sits a dog, who wakes me up with whining.

Cath. – Forbear! You both are bores, you've growled enough:
        No longer will I listen to such stuff!
        All men have nuisances and bores to afflict 'um:
        Hark then, and bow to my official dictum!

        For you, Johannes, there is most excuse,
        (Some interruptions are the very deuce)
        You're younger than the other cove, who surely
        Might have some sense – besides, you're somewhat poorly.
        This therefore is my sentence, that you nurse
        The Baby for seven hours, and nothing worse.

        For you, Edwardus, I shall say no more
        Than that your griefs are fudge, yourself a bore:
        Return at once to cold, stewed, minced, hashed mutton –
        To wristbands ever guiltless of a button –
        To raging winds and sea (where don't you wish
        Your luck may ever let you catch one fish?) –
        To make large drawings nobody will buy –
        To paint oil pictures which will never dry –
        To write new books which nobody will read –
        To drink weak tea, on tough old pigs to feed –
        Till spring-time brings the birds and leaves and flowers,
        And time restores a world of happier hours.   129

Calico Pie

Calico Pie,
The little Birds fly
Down to the calico tree,
Their wings were blue,
And they sang 'Tilly-loo!'
Till away they flew, –
And they never came back to me!
They never came back!
They never came back!
They never came back to me!

Calico Jam,
The little Fish swam,
Over the syllabub sea,
He took off his hat,
To the Sole and the Sprat,
And the Willeby-wat, –
But he never came back to me!
He never came back!
He never came back!
He never came back to me!

Calico Ban,
The little Mice ran,
To be ready in time for tea,
Flippity flup,
They drank it all up,
And danced in the cup, –
But they never came back to me!
They never came back!
They never came back!
They never came back to me!

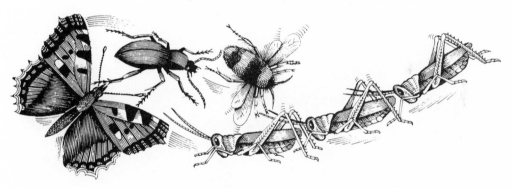

Calico Drum,
The Grasshoppers come,
The Butterfly, Beetle, and Bee,
Over the ground,
Around and round,
With a hop and a bound, –
But they never came back!
They never came back!
They never came back!
They never came back to me!

131

There was a Young Lady of Clare,
Who was sadly pursued by a bear;
When she found she was tired, she abruptly expired,
That unfortunate lady of Clare.

There was an Old Man who said, 'How,
– shall I flee from this horrible Cow?
I will sit on this stile, and continue to smile,
Which may soften the heart of that Cow.'

There was a Young Lady of Hull,
Who was chased by a virulent Bull;
But she seized on a spade, and called out – 'Who's afraid!'
Which distracted that virulent Bull.

There was an Old Person in black,
A Grasshopper jumped on his back;
When it chirped in his ear, he was smitten with fear,
That helpless Old Person in black.

133

There was an Old Man of Three Bridges,
Whose mind was distracted by midges,
He sate on a wheel, eating underdone veal,
Which relieved that Old Man of Three Bridges.

There was an Old Person of Dover,
Who rushed through a field of blue Clover;
But some very large bees, stung his nose and his knees,
So he very soon went back to Dover.

There was an Old Man of the Dee,
Who was sadly annoyed by a flea;
When he said, 'I will scratch it' – they gave him a hatchet,
Which grieved that Old Man of the Dee.

There was an Old Man of Quebec,
A beetle ran over his neck;
But he cried, 'With a needle, I'll slay you, O beadle!'
That angry Old Man of Quebec.

135

There lived a Small Puppy at Narkunda
Who sought for the best tree to bark under
Which he found, and said, 'Now, I can call out Bow Wow,
Underneath the best cedar in Narkunda.'

There was an Old Man of Narkunda,
Whose voice was like peals of loud thunder.
It shivered the hills into Colveynth pills,
And destroyed half the trees of Narkunda.

There was a Small Child at Narkunda,
Who said, 'Don't you hear, that is Thunder!'
But they said, 'It's the Bonzes amaking responses
In a temple eight miles from Narkunda.'

There was an Old Person of Paxo
Which complained when the fleas bit his back so,
But they gave him a chair, and impelled him to swear,
Which relieved that Old Person of Paxo.

There was an Old Person of Shoreham,
Whose habits were marked by decorum;
He bought an Umbrella, and sate in the cellar,
Which pleased all the people of Shoreham.

There was a Young Person of Ayr,
Whose head was remarkably square:
On the top, in fine weather, she wore a gold feather;
Which dazzled the people of Ayr.

There was an Old Person of Dutton,
Whose head was as small as a button:
So to make it look big, he purchased a wig,
And rapidly rushed about Dutton.

There was an Old Person of Woking,
Whose mind was perverse and provoking;
He sate on a rail, with his head in a pail,
That illusive Old Person of Woking.

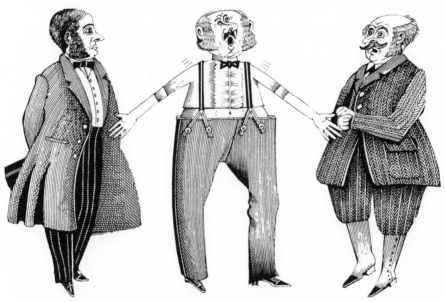

There was an Old Man who felt pert
When he wore a pale rose-coloured shirt.
When they said – 'Is it pleasant?' – he cried –
　　　　　　　　'Not at present –
It's a *leetle* too short – is my shirt!'

There was an Old Person of Cannes,
Who purchased three fowls and a fan;
Those she placed on a stool, and to make them feel cool
She constantly fanned them at Cannes.

There was an Old Person of Brigg,
Who purchased no end of a wig;
So that only his nose, and the end of his toes,
Could be seen when he walked about Brigg.

There was an Old Person of Mold,
Who shrank from sensations of cold;
So he purchased some muffs, some furs and some fluffs,
And wrapped himself from the cold.

There was a Young Lady of Dorking,
Who bought a large bonnet for walking;
But its colour and size, so bedazzled her eyes,
That she very soon went back to Dorking.

There was a Young Lady whose bonnet,
Came untied when the birds sate upon it;
But she said, 'I don't care! All the birds in the air
Are welcome to sit on my bonnet!'

There was an Old Man of Dee-side
Whose hat was exceedingly wide,
But he said, 'Do not fail, if it happen to hail
To come under my hat at Dee-side.'

There was an Old Man of Thames Ditton,
Who called for something to sit on;
But they brought him a hat, and said – 'Sit upon that,
You abruptious Old Man of Thames Ditton!'

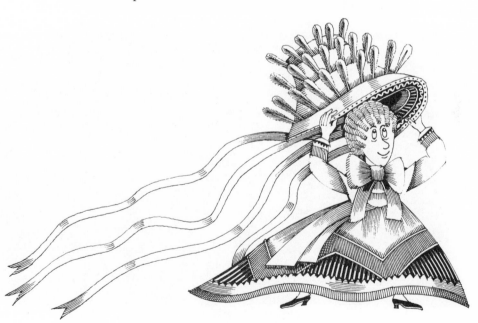

There was a Young Person in red,
Who carefully covered her head,
With a bonnet of leather, and three lines of feather,
Besides some long ribands of red.

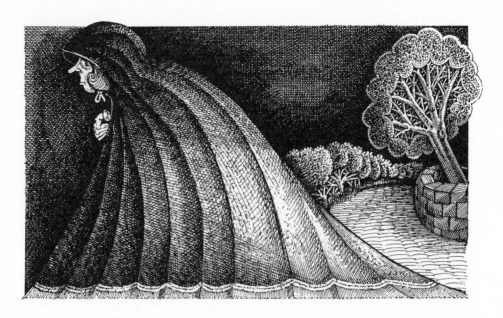

There was a Young Person in green,
Who seldom was fit to be seen;
She wore a long shawl, over bonnet and all,
Which enveloped that person in green.

There was an Old Person of Barnes,
Whose garments were covered with darns;
But they said, 'Without doubt, you will soon wear them out,
You luminous person of Barnes!'

There was an Old Person of Brill,
Who purchased a shirt with a frill;
But they said, 'Don't you wish, you may'nt look like a fish,
You obsequious Old Person of Brill?'

There was a Young Person of Crete,
Whose toilette was far from complete;
She dressed in a sack, spickle-speckled with black,
That ombliferous person of Crete.

There was an Old Man in a pew,
Whose waistcoat was spotted with blue;
But he tore it in pieces, to give to his nieces, –
That cheerful Old Man in a pew.

There was an Old Man of the West,
Who wore a pale plum-coloured vest;
When they said, 'Does it fit?' he replied, 'Not a bit!'
146   That uneasy Old Man of the West.

There was an Old Man of Blackheath,
Whose head was adorned with a wreath,
Of lobsters and spice, pickled onions and mice,
That uncommon Old Man of Blackheath.

There was an Old Person of Bude,
Whose deportment was vicious and crude;
He wore a large ruff, of pale straw-coloured stuff,
Which perplexed all the people of Bude.

There was an Old Person of Shields,
Who frequented the valley and fields;
All the mice and the cats, and the snakes and the rats,
Followed after that person of Shields.

There was an Old Man who supposed,
That the street door was partially closed;
But some very large rats, ate his coats and his hats,
While that futile old gentleman dozed.

There was an Old Man on a hill,
Who seldom, if ever, stood still;
He ran up and down, in his Grandmother's gown,
Which adorned that Old Man on a hill.

There was a Young Lady of Greenwich,
Whose garments were border'd with Spinach;
But a large spotty Calf, bit her shawl quite in half,
Which alarmed that Young Lady of Greenwich.

149

The New Vestments

There lived an Old Man in the Kingdom of Tess,
Who invented a purely original dress;
And when it was perfectly made and complete,
He opened the door, and walked into the street.

By way of a hat, he'd a loaf of Brown Bread,
In the middle of which he inserted his head; –
His Shirt was made up of no end of dead Mice,
The warmth of whose skins was quite fluffy and nice; –
His Drawers were of Rabbit-skins; – so were his Shoes; –
His Stockings were skins, – but it is not known whose; –
His Waistcoat and Trowsers were made of Pork Chops; –
His Buttons were Jujubes, and Chocolate Drops; –
His Coat was all Pancakes with Jam for a border,
And a girdle of Biscuits to keep it in order;
And he wore over all, as a screen from bad weather,
A Cloak of green Cabbage-leaves stitched all together.

He had walked a short way, when he heard a great noise,
Of all sorts of Beasticles, Birdlings, and Boys; –
And from every long street and dark lane in the town
Beasts, Birdles, and Boys in a tumult rushed down.
Two Cows and a half ate his Cabbage-leaf Cloak; –
Four Apes seized his Girdle, which vanished like smoke; –
Three Kids ate up half of his Pancakey Coat, –
And the tails were devour'd by an ancient He-Goat; –
An army of Dogs in a twinkling tore *up* his
Pork Waistcoat and Trowsers to give to their Puppies; –
And while they were growling, and mumbling the Chops,
Ten Boys prigged the Jujubes and Chocolate Drops. –

He tried to run back to his house, but in vain,
For Scores of fat Pigs came again and again; –
They rushed out of stables and hovels and doors, –
They tore off his stockings, his shoes, and his drawers; –
And now from the housetops with screechings descend,
Striped, spotted, white, black, and gray Cats without end,
They jumped on his shoulders and knocked off his hat, –
When Crows, Ducks, and Hens made a mincemeat of that; –
They speedily flew at his sleeves in a trice,
And utterly tore up his Shirt of dead Mice; –
They swallowed the last of his Shirt with a squall, –
Whereon he ran home with no clothes on at all.

And he said to himself as he bolted the door,
'I will not wear a similar dress any more,
Any more, any more, any more, never more!'

Mrs Jaypher

(To be read 'sententiously and with grave importance')

Mrs Jaypher found a wafer
Which she stuck upon a note;
This she took and gave the cook.
Then she went and bought a boat
Which she paddled down the stream
Shouting, 'Ice produces cream,
Beer when churned produces butter!
Henceforth all the words I utter
Distant ages thus shall note –
"From the Jaypher Wisdom-Boat."'

Mrs Jaypher said, 'it's safer
If you've lemons in your head;
First to eat, a pound of meat,
And then to go at once to bed.
Eating meat is half the battle,
Till you hear the Lemons rattle!
If you don't, you'll always moan;
In a Lemoncolly tone;
For there's nothing half so dreadful,
          as Lemons in your head!'

There was an Old Person of Deal
Who in walking, used only his heel;
When they said, 'Tell us why?' – he made no reply;
That mysterious Old Person of Deal.

There was an Old Man of Melrose,
Who walked on the tips of his toes;
But they said, 'It ain't pleasant, to see you at present,
154   You stupid Old Man of Melrose.'

There was an Old Man of Dumblane,
Who greatly resembled a crane;
But they said, – 'Is it wrong, since your legs are so long,
To request you won't stay in Dumblane?'

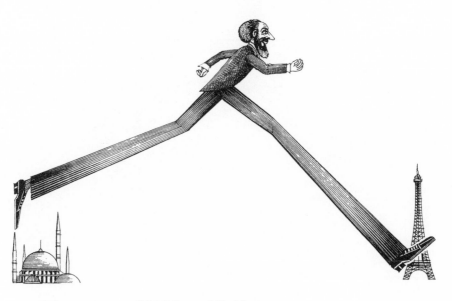

There was an Old Man of Coblenz,
The length of whose legs was immense;
He went with one prance, from Turkey to France,
That surprising Old Man of Coblenz.

155

There was an Old Person of Wilts,
Who constantly walked upon stilts;
He wreathed them with lilies, and daffy-down-dillies,
That elegant person of Wilts.

There was an Old Man of the Wrekin
Whose shoes made a horrible creaking;
But they said, 'Tell us whether, your shoes are of leather,
Or of what, you Old Man of the Wrekin?'

There was an Old Man of Toulouse
Who purchased a new pair of shoes;
When they asked, 'Are they pleasant?' – he said, 'Not at present!'
That turbid Old Man of Toulouse.

Incidents in the Life of my Uncle Arly

O my aged Uncle Arly!
Sitting on a heap of Barley
    Thro' the silent hours of night, –
Close beside a leafy thicket: –
On his nose there was a Cricket, –
In his hat a Railway-Ticket; –
    (But his shoes were far too tight).

Long ago, in youth, he squander'd
All his goods away, and wander'd
    To the Tiniskoop-hills afar.
There on golden sunsets blazing,
Every evening found him gazing, –
Singing, – 'Orb! You're quite amazing!
    How I wonder what you are!'

Like the ancient Medes and Persians,
Always by his own exertions
    He subsisted on those hills; –
Whiles, – by teaching children spelling, –
Or at times by merely yelling, –
Or at intervals by selling
    Propter's Nicodemus Pills.

Later, in his morning rambles
He perceived the moving brambles –
    Something square and white disclose; –
'Twas a First-class Railway-Ticket;
But, on stooping down to pick it
Off the ground, – a pea-green Cricket
    Settled on my uncle's Nose.

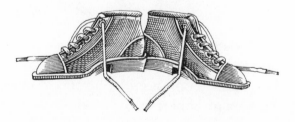

Never – never more, – oh! never,
Did that Cricket leave him ever, –
     Dawn or evening, day or night; –
Clinging as a constant treasure, –
Chirping with a cheerious measure, –
Wholly to my uncle's pleasure, –
     (Though his shoes were far too tight).

So for three-and-forty winters,
Till his shoes were worn to splinters,
     All those hills he wander'd o'er, –
Sometimes silent; – sometimes yelling; –
Till he came to Borley-Melling,
Near his old ancestral dwelling; –
     (But his shoes were far too tight).

On a little heap of Barley
Died my aged Uncle Arly,
     And they buried him one night; –
Close beside the leafy thicket; –
There, – his hat and Railway-Ticket; –
There, – his ever-faithful Cricket; –
     (But his shoes were far too tight).

She sits upon her Bulbul

She sits upon her Bulbul
Through the long, long hours of night –
And o'er the dark horizon gleams
The Yashmack's fitful light.
The lone Yaourt sails slowly down
The deep and craggy dell –
And from his lofty nest, loud screams
The white-plumed Asphodel.

O dear! How disgusting is life!

O dear! How disgusting is life!
To improve it O what can we do?
Most disgusting is hustle and strife,
and of all things an ill-fitting shoe –
shoe,
O bother an ill-fitting shoe!

Epitaph

'Beneath these high Cathedral stairs
Lie the remains of Susan Pares.
Her name was Wiggs, it was not Pares,
But Pares was put to rhyme with stairs.'

The Cummerbund

AN INDIAN POEM

She sate upon her Dobie,
   To watch the Evening Star,
And all the Punkahs as they passed,
   Cried, 'My! how fair you are!'
Around her bower, with quivering leaves,
   The tall Kamsamahs grew,
And Kitmutgars in wild festoons
   Hung down from Tchokis blue.

Below her home the river rolled
   With soft meloobious sound,
Where golden-finned Chuprassies swam,
   In myriads circling round.
Above, on tallest trees remote
   Green Ayahs perched alone,
And all night long the Mussak moan'd
   Its melancholy tone.

And where the purple Nullahs threw
   Their branches far and wide, –
And silvery Goreewallahs flew
   In silence, side by side, –
The little Bheesties' twittering cry
   Rose on the flagrant air,
And oft the angry Jampan howled
   Deep in his hateful lair.

She sate upon her Dobie, –
    She heard the Nimmak hum, –
When all at once a cry arose, –
    'The Cummerbund is come!'
In vain she fled: – with open jaws
    The angry monster followed,
And so (before assistance came)
    That Lady Fair was swollowed.

They sought in vain for even a bone
    Respectfully to bury, –
They said, – 'Hers was a dreadful fate!'
    (And Echo answered, 'Very.')
They nailed her Dobie to the wall,
    Where last her form was seen,
And underneath they wrote these words,
    In yellow, blue, and green: –

'Beware, ye Fair! Ye Fair, beware!
    Nor sit out late at night, –
Lest horrid Cummerbunds should come,
    And swollow you outright.'

The Daddy Long-legs and the Fly

Once Mr Daddy Long-legs,
   Dressed in brown and gray,
Walked about upon the sands
   Upon a summer's day;
And there among the pebbles,
   When the wind was rather cold,
He met with Mr Floppy Fly,
   All dressed in blue and gold.
And as it was too soon to dine,
They drank some Periwinkle-wine,
And played an hour or two, or more,
At battlecock and shuttledore.

Said Mr Daddy Long-legs
    To Mr Floppy Fly,
'Why do you never come to court?
    I wish you'd tell me why.
All gold and shine, in dress so fine,
    You'd quite delight the court.
Why do you never go at all?
    I really think you *ought*!
And if you went, you'd see such sights!
Such rugs! and jugs! and candle-lights!
And more than all, the King and Queen,
One in red, and one in green!'

'O Mr Daddy Long-legs,'
    Said Mr Floppy Fly,
'It's true I never go to court,
    And I will tell you why.
If I had six long legs like yours,
    At once I'd go to court!
But oh! I can't, because *my* legs
    Are so extremely short.
And I'm afraid the King and Queen
(One in red, and one in green)
Would say aloud, "You are not fit,
You Fly, to come to court a bit!"'

'O Mr Daddy Long-legs,'
  Said Mr Floppy Fly,
'I wish you'd sing one little song!
  One mumbian melody!
You used to sing so awful well
  In former days gone by,
But now you never sing at all;
  I wish you'd tell me why:
For if you would, the silvery sound
Would please the shrimps and cockles round,
And all the crabs would gladly come
To hear you sing, "Ah, Hum di Hum"!'

Said Mr Daddy Long-legs,
  'I can never sing again!
And if you wish, I'll tell you why,
  Although it gives me pain.
For years I cannot hum a bit,
  Or sing the smallest song;
And this the dreadful reason is,
  My legs are grown too long!
My six long legs, all here and there,
Oppress my bosom with despair;
And if I stand, or lie, or sit,
I cannot sing one single bit!'

So Mr Daddy Long-legs
  And Mr Floppy Fly
Sat down in silence by the sea,
  And gazed upon the sky.
They said, 'This is a dreadful thing!
The world has all gone wrong,
Since one has legs too short by half,
  The other much too long!
One never more can go to court,
Because his legs have grown too short;
The other cannot sing a song,
Because his legs have grown too long!'

Then Mr Daddy Long-legs
   And Mr Floppy Fly
Rushed downward to the foamy sea
   With one sponge-taneous cry;
And there they found a little boat,
   Whose sails were pink and gray;
And off they sailed among the waves,
   Far, and far away.
They sailed across the silent main,
And reached the great Gromboolian plain;
And there they play for evermore
At battlecock and shuttledore.

The Duck and the Kangaroo

Said the Duck to the Kangaroo,
  'Good gracious! how you hop!
Over the fields and the water too,
  As if you never would stop!
My life is a bore in this nasty pond,
And I long to go out in the world beyond!
  I wish I could hop like you!'
  Said the Duck to the Kangaroo.

'Please give me a ride on your back!'
  Said the Duck to the Kangaroo.
'I would sit quite still, and say nothing but "Quack,"
  The whole of the long day through!
And we'd go to the Dee, and the Jelly Bo Lee,
Over the land, and over the sea; –
  Please take me a ride! O do!'
  Said the Duck to the Kangaroo.

Said the Kangaroo to the Duck,
   'This requires some little reflection;
Perhaps on the whole it might bring me luck,
   And there seems but one objection,
Which is, if you'll let me speak so bold,
Your feet are unpleasantly wet and cold,
And would probably give me the roo-
   Matiz!' said the Kangaroo.

Said the Duck, 'As I sate on the rocks,
   I have thought over that completely,
And I bought four pairs of worsted socks
   Which fit my web-feet neatly.
And to keep out the cold I've bought a cloak,
And every day a cigar I'll smoke,
   All to follow my own dear true
   Love of a Kangaroo!'

Said the Kangaroo, 'I'm ready!
   All in the moonlight pale;
But to balance me well, dear Duck, sit steady!
   And quite at the end of my tail!'
So away they went with a hop and a bound,
And they hopped the whole world three times round;
   And who so happy, – O who,
   As the Duck and the Kangaroo?

The Table and the Chair

Said the Table to the Chair,
'You can hardly be aware,
How I suffer from the heat,
And from chilblains on my feet!
If we took a little walk,
We might have a little talk!
Pray let us take the air!'
Said the Table to the Chair.

Said the Chair unto the Table,
'Now you *know* we are not able!
How foolishly you talk,
When you know we *cannot* walk!'
Said the Table, with a sigh,
'It can do no harm to try,
I've as many legs as you,
Why can't we walk on two?'

So they both went slowly down,
And walked about the town
With a cheerful bumpy sound,
As they toddled round and round.
And everybody cried,
As they hastened to their side,
'See! The Table and the Chair
Have come out to take the air!'

But in going down an alley,
To a castle in a valley,
They completely lost their way,
And wandered all the day,
Till, to see them safely back,
They paid a Ducky-quack,
And a Beetle, and a Mouse,
Who took them to their house.

Then they whispered to each other,
'O delightful little brother!
What a lovely walk we've taken!
Let us dine on Beans and Bacon!'
So the Ducky, and the leetle
Browny-Mousy and the Beetle
Dined, and danced upon their heads
Till they toddled to their beds.

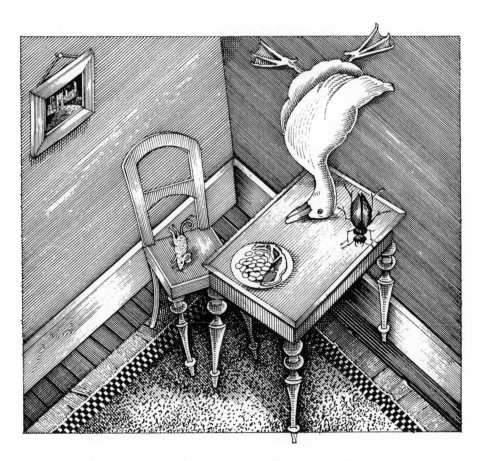

The Nutcrackers and the Sugar-tongs

The Nutcrackers sate by a plate on the table,
　　The Sugar-tongs sate by a plate at his side;
And the Nutcrackers said, 'Don't you wish we were able
　　Along the blue hills and green meadows to ride?
Must we drag on this stupid existence for ever,
　　So idle and weary, so full of remorse, –
While everyone else takes his pleasure, and never
　　Seems happy unless he is riding a horse?

'Don't you think we could ride without being instructed?
　　Without any saddle, or bridle, or spur?
Our legs are so long, and so aptly constructed,
　　I'm sure that an accident could not occur.
Let us all of a sudden hop down from the table,
　　And hustle downstairs, and each jump on a horse!
Shall we try? Shall we go? Do you think we are able?'
　　The Sugar-tongs answered distinctly, 'Of course!'

So down the long staircase they hopped in a minute,
    The Sugar-tongs snapped, and the Crackers said, 'Crack!'
The stable was open, the horses were in it;
    Each took out a pony, and jumped on his back.
The Cat in a fright scrambled out of the doorway,
    The Mice tumbled out of a bundle of hay,
The brown and white Rats, and the black ones from Norway,
    Screamed out, 'They are taking the horses away!'

The whole of the household was filled with amazement,
    The Cups and the Saucers danced madly about,
The Plates and the Dishes looked out of the casement,
    The Saltcellar stood on his head with a shout,
The Spoons with a clatter looked out of the lattice,
    The Mustard-pot climbed up the Gooseberry Pies,
The Soup-ladle peeped through a heap of Veal Patties,
    And squeaked with a ladle-like scream of surprise.

The Frying-pan said, 'It's an awful delusion!'
    The Tea-kettle hissed and grew black in the face;
And they all rushed downstairs in the wildest confusion,
    To see the great Nutcracker-Sugar-tong race.
And out of the stable, with screamings and laughter
    (Their ponies were cream-coloured, speckled with brown)
The Nutcrackers first, and the Sugar-tongs after,
    Rode all round the yard, and then all round the town.

They rode through the street, and they rode by the station,
    They galloped away to the beautiful shore;
In silence they rode, and 'made no observation',
    Save this: 'We will never go back any more!'
And still you might hear, till they rode out of hearing,
    The Sugar-tongs snap, and the Crackers say, 'Crack!'
Till far in the distance their forms disappearing,
    They faded away. – And they never came back!

The Broom, the Shovel, the Poker and the Tongs

The Broom and the Shovel, the Poker and Tongs,
   They all took a drive in the Park,
And they each sang a song, Ding-a-dong, Ding-a-dong,
   Before they went back in the dark.
Mr Poker he sate quite upright in the coach,
   Mr Tongs made a clatter and clash,
Miss Shovel was dressed all in black (with a brooch),
   Mrs Broom was in blue (with a sash).
      Ding-a-dong! Ding-a-dong!
      And they all sang a song!

'O Shovely so lovely!' the Poker he sang,
   'You have perfectly conquered my heart!
Ding-a-dong! Ding-a-dong! If you're pleased with my song,
   I will feed you with cold apple tart!
When you scrape up the coals with a delicate sound,
   You enrapture my life with delight!
Your nose is so shiny! your head is so round!
   And your shape is so slender and bright!
      Ding-a-dong! Ding-a-dong!
      Ain't you pleased with my song?'

'Alas! Mrs Broom!' sighed the Tongs in his song,
    'O is it because I'm so thin,
And my legs are so long – Ding-a-dong! Ding-a-dong!
    That you don't care about me a pin?
Ah! fairest of creatures, when sweeping the room,
    Ah! why don't you heed my complaint!
Must you needs be so cruel, you beautiful Broom,
    Because you are covered with paint?
        Ding-a-dong! Ding-a-dong!
        You are certainly wrong!'

Mrs Broom and Miss Shovel together they sang,
    'What nonsense you're singing today!'
Said the Shovel, 'I'll certainly hit you a bang!'
    Said the Broom, 'And I'll sweep you away!'
So the Coachman drove homeward as fast as he could,
    Perceiving their anger with pain;
But they put on the kettle, and little by little,
    They all became happy again.
        Ding-a-dong! Ding-a-dong!
        There's an end of my song!

Teapots and Quails,
Snuffers and Snails,
Set him a sailing
and see how he sails!

Mitres and Beams,
Thimbles and Creams,
Set him a screaming
and hark! how he screams!

Houses and Kings,
Whiskers and Swings,
Set him a stinging
and see how he stings!

Ribands and Pigs,
Helmets and Figs,
Set him a jigging
and see how he jigs!

Rainbows and Knives,
Muscles and Hives,
Set him a driving
and see how he drives!

Tadpoles and Tops,
Teacups and Mops,
Set him a hopping
and see how he hops!

Herons and Sweeps,
Turbans and Sheeps,
Set him a weeping
and see how he weeps!

Lobsters and Owls,
Scissors and Fowls,
Set him a howling
and hark how he howls!

Eagles and Pears,
Slippers and Bears,
Set him a staring
and see how he stares!

Sofas and Bees,
Camels and Keys,
Set him a sneezing
and see how he'll sneeze!

Wafers and Bears,
Ladders and Squares,
Set him a staring
and see how he stares!

Cutlets and Eyes,
Swallows and Pies,
Set it a flying
and see how it flies!

Thistles and Moles,
Crumpets and Soles,
Set it a rolling
and see how it rolls!

Tea urns and Pews,
Muscles and Jews,
Set him a mewing
and hear how he mews!

Watches and Oaks,
Custards and Cloaks,
Set him a poking
and see how he pokes!

Bonnets and Legs,
Steamboats and Eggs,
Set him a begging
and see how he begs!

Volumes and Pigs,
Razors and Figs,
Set him a jigging
and see how he jigs!

Hurdles and Mumps
Poodles and Pumps,
Set it a jumping
and see how he jumps!

Pancakes and Fins,
Roses and Pins,
Set him a grinning
and see how he grins!

Gruel and Prawns,
Bracelets and Thorns,
Set him a yawning
and see how he yawns!

Chimnies and Wings,
Sailors and Rings,
Set him a singing
and hark how he sings!

Trumpets and Guns,
Beetles and Buns,
Set him a running
and see how he runs!

Saucers and Tops,
Lobsters and Mops,
Set it a hopping
and see how he hops!

Puddings and Beams,
Cobwebs and Creams,
Set him a screaming
and hear how he screams!

Rainbows and Wives,
Puppies and Hives,
Set him a driving
and see how he drives!

Houses and Kings,
Oysters and Rings,
Set him a singing
and see how he sings!

Scissors and Fowls,
Filberts and Owls,
Set him a howling
and see how he howls!

Blackbirds and Ferns,
Spiders and Churns,
Set it a turning
and see how it turns!

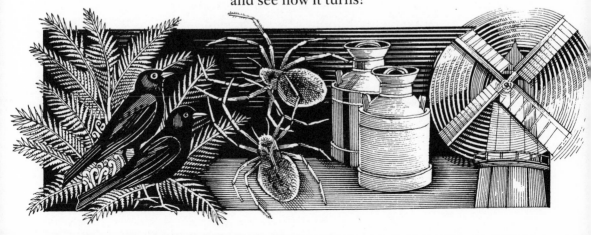

The Pelican Chorus

King and Queen of the Pelicans we;
No other Birds so grand we see!
None but we have feet like fins!
With lovely leathery throats and chins!
    Ploffskin, Pluffskin, Pelican jee!
    We think no Birds so happy as we!
    Plumpskin, Ploshkin, Pelican jill!
    We think so then, and we thought so still!

We live on the Nile. The Nile we love.
By night we sleep on the cliffs above;
By day we fish, and at eve we stand
On long bare islands of yellow sand.
And when the sun sinks slowly down
And the great rock walls grow dark and brown,
Where the purple river rolls fast and dim
And the Ivory Ibis starlike skim,
Wing to wing we dance around, –
Stamping our feet with a flumpy sound, –
Opening our mouths as Pelicans ought,
And this is the song we nightly snort; –
    Ploffskin, Pluffskin, Pelican jee, –
    We think no Birds so happy as we!
    Plumpskin, Ploshkin, Pelican jill, –
    We think so then, and we thought so still.

Last year came out our Daughter, Dell;
And all the Birds received her well.
To do her honour, a feast we made
For every bird that can swim or wade.
Herons and Gulls, and Cormorants black,
Cranes, and Flamingoes with scarlet back,
Plovers and Storks, and Geese in clouds,
Swans and Dilberry Ducks in crowds.
Thousands of Birds in wondrous flight!
They ate and drank and danced all night,
And echoing back from the rocks you heard
Multitude-echoes from Bird and Bird, –

Ploffskin, Pluffskin, Pelican jee,
We think no Birds so happy as we!
Plumpskin, Ploshkin, Pelican jill
We think so then, and we thought so still!

Yes, they came; and among the rest,
The King of the Cranes all grandly dressed.
Such a lovely tail! Its feathers float
Between the ends of his blue dress-coat;
With pea-green trowsers all so neat,
And a delicate frill to hide his feet, –
(For though no one speaks of it, everyone knows,
He has got no webs between his toes!)

As soon as he saw our Daughter Dell,
In violent love that Crane King fell, –
On seeing her waddling form so fair,
With a wreath of shrimps in her short white hair.
And before the end of the next long day,
Our Dell had given her heart away;
For the King of the Cranes had won that heart,
With a Crocodile's egg and a large fish-tart.
She vowed to marry the King of the Cranes,
Leaving the Nile for stranger plains;
And away they flew in a gathering crowd
Of endless birds in a lengthening cloud.

Ploffskin, Pluffskin, Pelican jee,
We think no Birds so happy as we!
Plumpskin, Ploshkin, Pelican jill,
We think so then, and we thought so still!

And far away in the twilight sky,
We heard them singing a lessening cry, –
Farther and farther till out of sight,
And we stood alone in the silent night!
Often since, in the nights of June,
We sit on the sand and watch the moon; –
She has gone to the great Gromboolian plain,
And we probably never shall meet again!
Oft, in the long still nights of June,
We sit on the rocks and watch the moon; –
She dwells by the streams of the Chankly Bore,
And we probably never shall see her more.

Ploffskin, Pluffskin, Pelican jee,
We think no Birds so happy as we!
Plumpskin, Ploshkin, Pelican jill,
We think so then, and we thought so still!

187

There was an Old Person of Pisa,
Whose daughters did nothing to please her;
She dressed them in gray, and banged them all day,
Round the walls of the city of Pisa.

There was an Old Man of Marseilles,
Whose daughters wore bottle-green veils;
They caught several Fish, which they put in a dish,
And sent to their Pa' at Marseilles.

188

There was an Old Person of China,
Whose daughters were Jiska and Dinah,
Amelia and Fluffy, Olivia and Chuffy,
And all of them settled in China.

There was an Old Man of Bohemia,
Whose daughter was christened Euphemia;
Till one day, to his grief, she married a thief,
Which grieved that Old Man of Bohemia.

There was an Old Man of the Cape,
Who possessed a large Barbary Ape;
But the Ape one dark night, set the house on a light,
Which surprised that Old Man of the Cape.

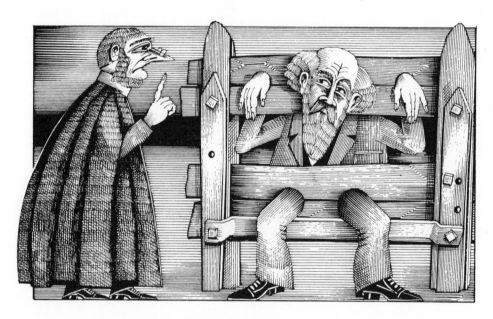

There was an Old Person of Cheadle,
Was put in the stocks by the beadle;
For stealing some pigs, some coats and some wigs,
That horrible person of Cheadle.

There was an Old Person of Gretna,
Who rushed down the crater of Etna;
When they said, 'Is it hot?' he replied, 'No, it's not!'
That mendacious Old Person of Gretna.

There was an Old Person of Hove,
Who frequented the depths of a grove;
Where he studied his books, with the wrens and the rooks,
That tranquil Old Person of Hove.

There was a Young Person whose history,
Was always considered a mystery;
She sate in a ditch, although no one knew which,
And composed a small treatise on history.

There was an Old Man of Vesuvius,
Who studied the works of Vitruvius;
When the flames burnt his book, to drinking he took,
That morbid Old Man of Vesuvius.

There was an Old Person of Cromer,
Who stood on one leg to read Homer;
When he found he grew stiff, he jumped over the cliff,
Which concluded that person of Cromer.

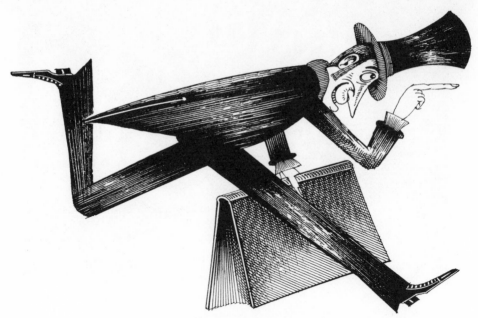

There was an Old Man with a book,
Who said, 'Only look! Only look! –
Osquation, Obsgration – at Waterloo Station –
Enquire if there ain't such a book!'

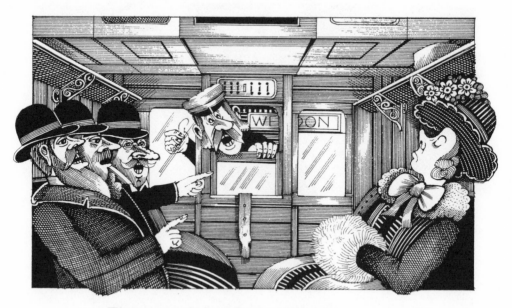

There was a Young Lady of Sweden,
Who went by the slow train to Weedon;
When they cried, 'Weedon Station!' she made no observation,
But she thought she should go back to Sweden.

194

There was an Old Man at a junction,
Whose feelings were wrung with compunction,
When they said, 'The Train's gone!' he exclaimed, 'How forlorn!'
But remained on the rails of the junction.

There was an Old Man at a station,
Who made a promiscuous oration;
But they said, 'Take some snuff! – you have talk'd quite enough
You afflicting Old Man at a station!'

Dingle Bank

He lived at Dingle Bank – he did; –
    He lived at Dingle Bank;
And in his garden was one Quail,
    Four tulips, and a Tank:
And from his windows he could see
The otion and the River Dee.

His house stood on a Cliff, – it did,
    Its aspic it was cool;
And many thousand little boys
    Resorted to his school,
Where if of progress they could boast
He gave them heaps of buttered toast.

But he grew rabid-wroth, he did,
    If they neglected books,
And dragged them to adjacent Cliffs
    With beastly Button Hooks,
And there with fatuous glee he threw
Them down into the otion blue.

And in the sea they swam, they did, –
    All playfully about,
And some eventually became
    Sponges, or speckled trout: –
But Liverpool doth all bewail
Their Fate; – likewise his Garden Quail.

The Octopods and Reptiles

The Octopods and Reptiles,
They dine at 6 o'clock,
And having dined rush wildly out
Like an electric shock.
They hang about the bannisters
The corridors they block
And gabbling bothering
A most unpleasant flock.
They hang about the bannisters
Upon the stairs they flock
And howly-gabbling all the while
The corridors they block.

The Uncareful Cow

The Uncareful Cow, she walked about,
But took no care at all;
And so she bumped her silly head
Against a hard stone wall.
And when the bump began to grow
Into a Horn, they said –
'There goes the Uncareful Cow, – who has
Three Horns upon her head!'

And when the Bumpy Horn grew large,
'Uncareful Cow!' – they said –
'Here, take and hang the Camphor bottle
Upon your bumpy head! –
And with the Camphor rub the bump
Two hundred times a day,!' –
And so she did – till bit by bit
She rubbed the Horn away.

An unfinished limerick

There was an Old Man who said, 'Now
I'll sit on the horns of that cow.'

There was an Old Person of Rhodes,
Who strongly objected to toads;
He paid several cousins, to catch them by dozens,
That futile Old Person of Rhodes.

There was a Young Lady of Troy,
Whom several large flies did annoy;
Some she killed with a thump, some she drowned at the pump,
And some she took with her to Troy.

There was an Old Person of Twickenham,
Who whipped his four horses to quicken 'em;
When they stood on one leg, he said faintly, 'I beg
We may go back directly to Twickenham!'

There was a Young Person of Smyrna,
Whose Grandmother threatened to burn her;
But she seized on the Cat, and said, 'Granny, burn that!
You incongruous Old Woman of Smyrna!'

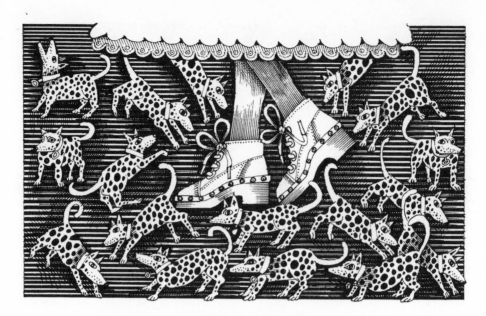

There was a Young Lady of Ryde,
Whose shoe-strings were seldom untied;
She purchased some clogs, and some small spotty dogs,
And frequently walked about Ryde.

There was an Old Man of Kamschatka,
Who possessed a remarkably fat cur.
His gait and his waddle, were held as a model,
To all the fat dogs in Kamschatka.

There was an Old Man of Ancona,
Who found a small dog with no owner,
Which he took up and down, all the streets of the town;
That anxious Old Man of Ancona.

There was an Old Man of Leghorn,
The smallest as ever was born;
But quickly snapt up he, was once by a puppy,
Who devoured that Old Man of Leghorn.

203

There was a Young Lady of Bute,
Who played on a silver-gilt flute;
She played several jigs, to her uncle's white pigs,
That amusing Young Lady of Bute.

There was an Old Man with a flute,
A sarpint ran into his boot;
But he played day and night, till the sarpint took flight,
And avoided that man with a flute.

There was a Young Lady of Welling,
Whose praise all the world was a telling;
She played on the harp, and caught several carp,
That accomplished Young Lady of Welling.

There was a Young Lady whose chin,
Resembled the point of a pin;
So she had it made sharp, and purchased a harp,
And played several tunes with her chin.

There was an Old Man in a marsh,
Whose manners were futile and harsh;
He sate on a log, and sang songs to a frog,
That instructive Old Man in a marsh.

There was an Old Person of Bradley
Who sang all so loudly and sadly;
With a poker and tongs, he beat time to his songs,
That melodious Old Person of Bradley!

There was a Young Lady of Tyre,
Who swept the loud chords of a lyre;
At the sound of each sweep, she enraptured the deep,
And enchanted the city of Tyre.

There was an Old Person of Cheam,
Who said, 'It is just like a dream,
When I play on the drum, and wear rings on my thumb
In the beautiful meadows of Cheam!'

There was an Old Person of Jodd,
Whose ways were perplexing and odd;
She purchased a whistle, and sate on a thistle,
And squeaked to the people of Jodd.

There was an Old Person of Bray,
Who sang through the whole of the day
To his ducks and his pigs, whom he fed upon figs,
That valuable person of Bray.

There was an Old Person of Dundalk,
Who tried to teach fishes to walk;
When they tumbled down dead, he grew weary, and said,
'I had better go back to Dundalk!'

There was an Old Man of Dumbree,
Who taught little owls to drink tea;
For he said, 'To eat mice, is not proper or nice',
That amiable man of Dumbree.

There was an Old Man of Apulia,
Whose conduct was very peculiar;
He fed twenty sons, upon nothing but buns,
That whimsical man of Apulia.

There was an Old Person of Sparta,
Who had twenty-five sons and one daughter;
He fed them on snails, and weighed them in scales,
That wonderful person of Sparta.

There was an Old Man of the East,
Who gave all his children a feast;
But they all ate so much, and their conduct was such,
That it killed that Old Man of the East.

There was a Young Person of Bantry,
Who frequently slept in the pantry;
When disturbed by the mice, she appeased them with rice,
That judicious Young Person of Bantry.

There was a Young Lady of Wales,
Who caught a large fish without scales;
When she lifted her hook, she exclaimed, 'Only look!'
That ecstatic Young Lady of Wales.

There was an Old Person of Bree,
Who frequented the depths of the sea;
She nurs'd the small fishes, and washed all the dishes,
And swam back again into Bree.

There was an Old Man of the Dargle
Who purchased six barrels of Gargle;
For he said, 'I'll sit still, and will roll them down hill,
For the fish in the depths of the Dargle.'

There was an Old Person in gray,
Whose feelings were tinged with dismay;
She purchased two parrots, and fed them with carrots,
Which pleased that Old Person in gray.

There was a Young Lady of Corsica,
Who purchased a little brown saucy-cur;
Which she fed upon ham, and hot raspberry jam,
That expensive Young Lady of Corsica.

There was an Old Man of the Hague,
Whose ideas were excessively vague;
He built a balloon, to examine the moon,
That deluded Old Man of the Hague.

The Youthful Cove

Once on a time a youthful cove
    As was a cheery lad
Lived in a villa by the sea –
    The cove was not so bad;

The dogs and cats, the cows and ass,
    The birds in cage or grove
The rabbits, hens, ducks, pony, pigs
    All loved that cheery lad.

Seven folks – one female and six male, –
    Seized on that youthful cove;
They said – 'To edjukate this chap
    Us seven it doth behove.'

The first his parrient was, – who taught
    The cove to read and ride,
Latin, and Grammarithemetic,
    And lots of things beside.

Says Pa, 'I'll spare no pains or time
    Your schools hours so to cut,
And square and fit, that you will make
    No end of progress – *but* –,'

Says Mrs Grey, – 'I'll teach him French,
    Pour parler dans cette pays –
Je cris, qu'il parlera bien,
    Même comme un Français – *Mais* –'

Says Signor Gambinossi, – 'Si
    Progresso si farà,
Lo voglio insegnare qui,
    La lingua mia, – ma,' –

Says Mr Grump – 'Geology,
   And Mathetics stiff
I'll teach the cove, who's sure to go
   Ahead like blazes, – *if* –'

Says James – 'I'll teach him everyday
   My Nastics: now and then
To stand upon his 'ed; and make
   His mussels harder, – when' –

Says Signor Blanchi, – 'Lascia far; –
   La musica da me,
Ben insegnata qli serà; –
   Farà progresso, – *Se* –'

Says Edmund Lear – 'I'll make him draw
   A Palace, or a hut,
Trees, mountains, rivers, cities, plains,
   And p'rapps to paint them – *but* –'

So all these 7 joined hands and sang
   This chorus by the sea; –
'O! Ven his edjukation's done,
   By! Vot a cove he'll be!'

The Scroobious Pip

The Scroobious Pip went out one day
When the grass was green, and the sky was grey.
Then all the Beasts in the world came round
When the Scroobious Pip sat down on the ground.

       The cat and the dog and the kangaroo
       The sheep and the cow and the guineapig too
       The wolf he howled, the horse he neighed
       The little pig squeaked and the donkey brayed
       And when the lion began to roar
       There never was heard such a noise before.
       And every Beast he stood on the tip
       Of his toes to look at the Scroobious Pip.
At last they said to the Fox – 'By far,
You're the wisest Beast! You know you are!
Go close to the Scroobious Pip and say,
Tell us all about yourself we pray –
For as yet we can't make out in the least
If you're Fish or Insect, or Bird or Beast.'
The Scroobious Pip looked vaguely round
And sang these words with a rumbling sound –
       Chippetty Flip; Flippetty Chip; –
My only name is the Scroobious Pip.

The Scroobious Pip from the top of a tree
Saw the distant Jellybolee, –
And all the Birds in the world came there,
Flying in crowds all through the air.

       The vulture and eagle, the cock and the hen
       The ostrich the turkey the snipe and the wren
       The parrot chattered, the blackbird sung
       And the Owl looked wise but held his tongue,
       And when the Peacock began to scream
       The hullabaloo was quite extreme.
       And every Bird he fluttered the tip
       Of his wing as he stared at the Scroobious Pip.
At last they said to the Owl – 'By far,
You're the wisest Bird – you know you are!

Fly close to the Scroobious Pip and say,
Explain all about yourself we pray –
For as yet we have neither seen nor heard
If you're Fish or Insect, Beast or Bird!'
The Scroobious Pip looked gaily round
And sang these words with a chirpy sound –
        Flippetty chip – Chippetty flip –
My only name is the Scroobious Pip.

The Scroobious Pip went into the sea
By the beautiful shore of the Jellybolee –
All the Fish in the world swam round
With a splashing squashy spluttering sound.
        The sprat, the herring, the turbot too
        The shark the sole and the mackerel blue,
        The flounder sputtered, the porpoise puffed

        And when the Whale began to spout

        And every Fish he shook the tip
        Of his tail as he gazed on the Scroobious Pip.
At last they said to the Whale – 'By far
You're the biggest Fish – you know you are!
Swim close to the Scroobious Pip and say –
Tell us all about yourself we pray! –
For to know you yourself is our only wish;
Are you Beast or Insect, Bird or Fish?'
The Scroobious Pip looked softly round
And sung these words with a liquid sound –
        Pliffity flip, Pliffity flip –
My only name is the Scroobious Pip.

The Scroobious Pip sat under a tree
By the silent shores of the Jellybolee;
All the Insects in all the world
About the Scroobious Pip entwirled.
Beetles and  with purple eyes
Gnats and buzztilential flies –
Grasshoppers, butterflies, spiders too,
Wasps and bees and dragon-flies blue,
And when the gnats began to hum
bounced like a dismal drum,
And every Insect curled the tip
Of his snout, and looked at the Scroobious Pip.
At last they said to the Ant – 'By far
You're the wisest Insect, you know you are!
Creep close to the Scroobious Pip and say –
Tell us all about yourself we pray,
For we can't find out, and we can't tell why –
If you're Beast or Fish or a Bird or a Fly.'
The Scroobious Pip turned quickly round
And sang these words with a whistly sound
Wizzeby wip – wizzeby wip –
My only name is the Scroobious Pip.

Then all the Beasts that walk on the ground
Danced in a circle round and round –
And all the Birds that fly in the air
Flew round and round in a circle there,
And all the Fish in the Jellybolee
Swum in a circle about the sea,
And all the Insects that creep or go
Buzzed in a circle to and fro.
And they roared and sang and whistled and cried
Till the noise was heard from side to side –
Chippetty tip! Chippetty tip!
Its only name is the Scroobious Pip.

Spots of Greece

Papa once went to Greece,
   And there I understand
He saw no end of lovely spots
   About that lovely land.
He talks about these spots of Greece
   To both Mama and me
Yet spots of Greece upon my dress
   They can't abear to see!
I cannot make it out at all –
   If ever on my Frock
They see the smallest Spot of Greece
   It gives them quite a shock!
Henceforth, therefore, – to please them both
   These spots of Greece no more
Shall be upon my Frock at all –
   Nor on my Pinafore.

And this is certain

And this is certain; if so be
You could just now my garden see,
The aspic of my flowers so bright
Would make you shudder with delight.

And if you voz to see my roziz
As is a boon to all men's noziz, –
You'd fall upon your back and scream –
'O Lawk! O criky! It's a dream!'

O Mummery!

'O mummery! Torcher me know more!
The present's all or-cast.
My opes of fewther bliss is or –
In mussey-spare the past!'

Cold are the Crabs

Cold are the crabs that crawl on yonder hills,
Colder the cucumbers that grow beneath,
And colder still the brazen chops that wreathe
    The tedious gloom of philosophic pills!
For when the tardy film of nectar fills
The ample bowls of demons and of men,
There lurks the feeble mouse, the homely hen,
    And there the porcupine with all her quills.
Yet much remains – to weave a solemn strain
That lingering sadly – slowly dies away,
Daily departing with departing day.
A pea-green gamut on a distant plain
When wily walrusses in congress meet –
    Such such is life –

The Self-Portrait of the Laureate of Nonsense

How pleasant to know Mr Lear!
  Who has written such volumes of stuff!
Some think him ill-tempered and queer,
  But a few think him pleasant enough.

His mind is concrete and fastidious,
  His nose is remarkably big;
His visage is more or less hideous,
  His beard it resembles a wig.

He has ears, and two eyes, and ten fingers,
  Leastways if you reckon two thumbs;
Long ago he was one of the singers,
  But now he is one of the dumbs.

He sits in a beautiful parlour,
  With hundreds of books on the wall;
He drinks a great deal of Marsala,
  But never gets tipsy at all.

He has many friends, laymen and clerical;
  Old Foss is the name of his cat;
His body is perfectly spherical,
  He weareth a runcible hat.

When he walks in a waterproof white,
  The children run after him so!
Calling out, 'He's come out in his night-
  Gown, that crazy old Englishman, oh!'

He weeps by the side of the ocean,
  He weeps on the top of the hill;
He purchases pancakes and lotion,
  And chocolate shrimps from the mill.

He reads but he cannot speak Spanish,
  He cannot abide ginger-beer:
Ere the days of his pilgrimage vanish,
  How pleasant to know Mr Lear!

SOURCES

Books by Edward Lear published during his lifetime

A Book of Nonsense, Thomas McLean, London, 1846
Nonsense Songs, Stories, Botany and Alphabets, Robert Bush, London, 1871
More Nonsense, Pictures, Rhymes, Botany, &c, Robert Bush, London, 1872
Laughable Lyrics, A Fourth Book of Nonsense Poems, Songs, Botany, Music, &c,
   Robert Bush, London, 1877

Books published posthumously

Nonsense Songs and Stories, introduced by Sir Edward Strachey, Frederick
   Warne, London, 1894
Macmillan's Magazine, recorded by Edmund Lushington, April 1897
Letters of Edward Lear, edited by Lady Strachey, T. Fisher Unwin, London,
   1907
Later Letters of Edward Lear, edited by Lady Strachey, T. Fisher Unwin,
   London, 1911
Queery Leary Nonsense, edited by Lady Strachey, Mills & Boon, London, 1911
Edward Lear on My Shelves, edited by Bertha C. Slade for William B. Osgood
   Field, privately printed in New York, 1933
Edward Lear: Landscape Painter and Nonsense Poet, Angus Davidson, John
   Murray, London, 1938
Teapots and Quails and Other New Nonsenses by Edward Lear, edited and
   introduced by Angus Davidson and Philip Hofer, John Murray, London,
   1953
Edward Lear's Indian Journal, edited by Ray Murphy, Jarrolds Ltd, London,
   1953
Edward Lear as a Landscape Draughtsman, Philip Hofer, Oxford University
   Press, 1967
Edward Lear: the Life of a Wanderer, Vivien Noakes, Collins, London, 1968
Lear in the Original, introduction and notes by Herman W. Liebert, Oxford
   University Press, 1975
For Lovers of Flowers and Gardens: Edward Lear, compiled by Vivien Noakes and
   Charles Lewsen, Collins, London, 1978
For Lovers of Food and Drink: Edward Lear, compiled by Vivien Noakes and
   Charles Lewsen, Collins, London, 1978

INDEX OF TITLES AND FIRST LINES

Titles are given in italics. For the longer poems in the index the first line is only shown if it differs substantially from the title. The indexing of the limericks is based on the last word in the first line.